Psychic Senses

AN ESSENTIAL GUIDE TO DEVELOPING YOUR PSYCHIC AND MEDIUM GIFTS

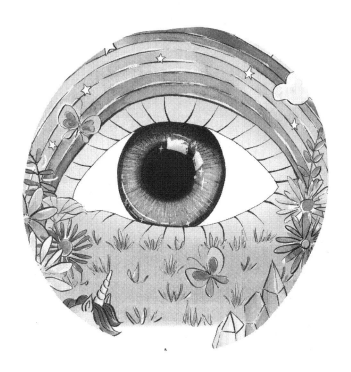

COLBY REBEL

The information in this book is intended as a guide for starting and building your own spiritual practice. Neither the author, Publishing or anyone associated with Psychic Senses claim it is a substitute for professional or medical services.

Cover Design: Georgi Petrov

Cover Illustration: Lizzie Martell & Rebecca Peitz

Book layout by Logotecture

ISBN-13: 978-0-578-55237-8
ISBN-10: 0-578-55237-X

Psychic Senses

An Essential Guide To Developing Your Psychic and Medium Gifts

COLBY REBEL

Message from Spirit

"Each of you has a light that shines from deep within your soul. We ask that you show that light and embrace one another with the kindness and compassion that we instilled in you from inception. You are a beautiful being meant to clear your mind of worry, despair and doubt. You are capable of anything you want so we ask that you want goodness. We ask that you go for greatness.

Know that you are such a beautiful blessing to those around you. Each person we put in your path is meant to experience your light. You have the ability to change the energy around you simply by stepping into your greatness. Your greatness of love is all that you need.

When you feel concern and worry, simply look within and trust us. Pull the light from within and let it cascade out so that you feel our warmth and *remember that we have never left you. We are within you.*

Start your journey knowing you already have it all. We have given you everything you need for happiness. It sits within you and when you doubt, go within and trust. Trust that you have the power to make a difference and to shine your light on others so that they too, can find the light within. With each connection you spark, your light will grow brighter and brighter. For one is now one-thousand.

When you use your light to help another find theirs, you are serving us. We send you out to the world so that you may see how much you are needed and how beautiful your light shines. We ask that you now take the time to look within and cast your light outwards, for they are one and the same."

-Spirit

Preface

Did you grow up struggling to understand your gift? Did you even realize you had a gift at all? Most likely, you just knew you were "different." While you may have had "imaginary friends," or dreams or premonitions that came true, no one ever sat you down to explain what was happening. You may have felt like an outsider or were teased by spiteful peers. In an effort to acclimate to the world around you, you dimmed your light and shut down your gifts or at the very minimum, kept them a secret from those around you.

Now is the time to turn your light back on. Although, you may have not had anyone to turn to or any resource to develop your gifts, you do now. This book was written to help *you*, the developing lightworker looking to deepen your connection, build your accuracy and trust your connection with spirit.

This book is filled with easy to understand explanations and practical exercises to help you develop your intuitive, psychic and medium skills.

You are a unique individual with a special gift. It's time to own it and step into your calling with confidence. Knowing that you are unique and special will keep you motivated when you experience self-doubt. Accepting your gift and embracing your individuality will allow the world to see you in the same light that Spirit does.

"Family isn't always blood. It's the people in your life who want you in theirs; the ones who accept you for who you are. The ones that would do anything to see you smile and who love you no matter what."

- Maya Angelou.

This book is dedicated to my family and best friend Renea. I am truly grateful for your unconditional love and support. Thank you for the countless hours you have volunteered, driven me and dealt with my anxiety to help me live my purpose. You are truly a blessing in my life. I am forever grateful.

Part 1 : Basics

Part 2 : Essentials

Part 3 : Deeper Details

Part 4 : Responsibilities

Acknowledgements

It's always difficult to express in words the positive impact that others can have on you. I have been blessed with so many people in my life that spirit has given me to help me on this path of service. Here's just a few that I'd like to express my deepest gratitude to for everything they've done to help me on this remarkable journey.

Family and friends,
I have been blessed by the best when it comes to family and friends. I want to again, thank my incredible family *Jane, Cheryl, Karen, Beverly, Leah, Kim, Angela,* and *Kristen* for their relentless dedication to this endeavor of Spirit and to my best friend *Renea* who believed in me from the very beginning of this extraordinary journey. Thank you to *Jennifer Shaffer* and *Michelle Eddins*. Your love and loyalty have meant more to me than I will ever

be able to adequately express. Thank you all from the bottom of my heart.

My teacher and friend Lisa Williams,
It has been an absolute privilege being a part of your LWISSD team as a Master Teacher and having the incredible honor of working with you for so many years. Thank you for believing in me and reassuring me at all of those nervous crossroads. Thank you for taking every call, answering every text and for always having my back. I love the pushes, the pulls and especially your *Mama Bear* hugs. I am forever grateful for your encouragement, and support. You are truly amazing.

Thank You Tutors,
Having the support of master teachers and peers is invaluable. For every tutor that stood with me in demonstration, I am humbled and honored. To every professional that agreed to be a guest on my podcast, *eternally* grateful. Although this is just naming a few of the great many, I wanted to express my deep gratitude to *Paul Jacobs, Chris Drew, Melinda Kushner, Mavis Pittilla, Jose Gosschalk,*

Andy Byng, Rhys Wynn Davies, Janet Nohavek, Joseph Shiel, Austyn Wells, Sue Williams and *Tony Stockwell*. Each of you has supported me on my path and has given me invaluable insight that I will cherish forever.

Fellow Colleagues and friends,
There are simply too many to name, but you *know* who you are! *Thank you* for volunteering at the monthly Spirit Service, for coming to the events, supporting the center, the community and students. Special thanks to *Jules Davis* for your friendship, support and social outings when desperately needed.

Students and Clients,
Without the students and clients there is no book to write. I have had the most amazing clients and students anyone fortunate enough to call this a career can have. I have learned so much from every student and have enjoyed witnessing their growth. To this day nothing brings more joy than watching them spread their wings and take their own *Leap of Faith*. Thank you to every client who has ever

entrusted me with the privilege of connecting to your loved ones in Spirit.

With Gratitude,

Colby

Introduction

Do you feel you have intuitive, psychic or medium gifts? Would you like to understand them better? Ready to explore the world of intuition, psychic and mediumship?

Welcome to Psychic Senses. The first book of its kind to provide clear and simple explanations to the psychic and medium connections as well as offering a compilation of exercises to help you hone your gifts.

Although there are many workshops, webinars and classes that offer instruction on developing your gifts. Few resources are dedicated to the sole purpose of offering a clear understanding of how psychic, mediumship and intuition connections work.

This book will provide you with essential and powerful exercises to help you develop your gifts naturally and easily.

Each exercise is designed with a precise intention to help you accomplish a particular task. Within the exercise, you will discover an opportunity to isolate and strengthen a specific sense. Take each exercise slowly and be sure to practice it several times. In fact, you can even make the exercises as part of your daily routine.

Repetition is a key component in developing your gifts. It's not as simple as a one and done endeavor. Development takes time, effort and commitment. There will be times when you will need to work on your inner self before you can move on to the next step.

Part of developing your gifts is also developing your soul. We are all here to learn, grow and expand. It's a beautiful balance between living a purposeful physical experience and honoring our inner spirit being. Ready to begin? Let's get started!

PART 1

Basics

CHAPTER 1 |
WHAT IS INTUITION?

The power or faculty of attaining to direct knowledge or cognition without evident rational thought and inference

-*Merriam Webster Dictionary*

We all have intuition. It's that gut feeling in the pit of your stomach that gives you a signal. This may be a forewarning. For example, you have an unexplained feeling or sensation that danger is ahead. It's also commonly referred to as getting a *hunch* or "Mother's Intuition". A mother just knows when something is amiss with her child. The feelings you receive are your natural gifts and they are derived from your sense of *feeling*.

Intuition stems from the unconscious mind and you don't consciously focus on receiving the information.

How many times have you driven down a road and for some reason had a feeling you should turn off early to take a different route home?

Instead, you ignore your initial instinct and proceed on route (because your car's GPS told you) to only discover there is construction ahead, thus creating a 30-minute delay! UGH! If you had only listened to your gut in the first place you wouldn't be stuck in bumper-to-bumper traffic!

This is your *INTUITION*.

Your intuition is *ALWAYS* right. It never leads you astray. You only tend to get into trouble when you proceed to process the information through your logical mind.

You may second-guess the initial feeling or thought dismissing it simply for your imagination. When you begin to trust your intuition as your compass of guidance, you can navigate your life in a way that is in alignment with your higher self.

How do you know if it's your own mind chatter or higher-self giving you the information? The best way to explain is that intuition will randomly POP in without notice. You may be thinking of something completely different and yet this "flash" of information comes in without notice. This is your intuitive, i.e. higher self. When you have a thought that slowly creeps in and continues to twirl around and fester with you and tends to be more fearful, this is usually your logical mind or ego. The thought will be slower and repetitive. This is your little ego voice.

How do you practice your intuition? First and foremost, TRUST what you receive!

1. Play Text Tag:
On your phone, remove all special rings and pings for your contacts. Then as you hear a message or call come through, see if you can intuitively tap into who is trying to contact you. Keep score of your success rate!

2. Take a Number:

Take blank sheets of paper and write a number on them. Turn them over and mix them around. Then place your hand on random sheets and tune in to see if you can accurately guess what number is on the other side.

3. Practice the Compass (coming up a later).

4. Office Attitude:

When you go to work, before stepping through the door to start your shift, tune into the atmosphere. Is your boss in a good mood? How is the energy? Practice your intuition each work day!

"Practice listening to your intuition, your inner voice; ask questions; be curious; see what you see; hear what you hear; and then act upon what you know to be true. These intuitive powers were given to your soul at birth."

— Clarissa Pinkola Estés, <u>Women Who Run With the Wolves: Myths and Stories of the Wild Woman Archetype</u>

CHAPTER 2 |
PSYCHIC CONNECTIONS

Sensitive to nonphysical or supernatural forces and influences: marked by extraordinary or mysterious sensitivity, perception, or understanding.

—Merriam Webster Dictionary

We all have intuition, but what is a psychic connection? A psychic connection is a soul- to-soul connection. My soul to your soul. When we keep it that simple, there is the ability to speak to someone's soul directly. Psychic is a high sense of awareness and vibration that helps link the information in a logical way. Some people have naturally "heightened senses". These senses can include any one or all of the following: seeing, hearing, feeling, tasting, smelling and knowing. Naturally, these sensations are then followed by a logical thought or premonition. For instance, a thought may a word. Perhaps it's just a quick feeling about something, but then you will see it connect to a person or related to a particular situation. When you get the hit of information *AND* you connect it to a person, place or situation in a logical way, *THAT* is using your psychic gifts!

For example, you see an old friend and a thought pops into your mind "she's going to be pregnant this year". In a few months she calls you to break the good news.   She is indeed expecting! There was nothing in her physical appearance when you saw her last that gave this away. It was a feeling that popped in followed by the logical thought "pregnant". You may have seen an image that flashed into your mind's eye of her pregnant or heard a voice that gave you the premonition. Either way, you received an impulse followed by a logical thought. The A+B=C is what establishes the psychic sense.

When you tune into another's soul you must have your vibration higher and awareness expanded. Literally, start by opening your heart. You will be creating a safe place to allow your sitter or recipient to open their heart in return.

As for tuning into ourselves, we all have the ability to speak to our own soul. Meditation helps tremendously with this. We all have the ability to connect to our own higher self, but sometimes we get stuck or we're in a funk or our vibration is low. This is where the practice of meditation comes in.

There are persons with extrasensory perception. For example, you may have the gift of hearing sound that goes beyond the physical realm. You may hear this in your inner ear. It will feel like your own imagination. The same is true for seeing. For instance, you see a flash or a movie, but it's within your imagination (not through the lens of your physical eye). These extrasensory senses are the tools needed for both psychic and medium connections.

When an impulse of information comes in, it's known as a "hit" of information. Have you ever had a vivid dream of an event or circumstance that then comes true? This is a premonition! Psychic "hits" come in various forms. It's truly a type of language, except rather than the language only being in the form of words, it is a language built on the unseen or unknown. The more we learn this language, the more we can communicate.

Tracking your premonitions is a great way to determine the timeline of what you are receiving. Purchase a journal and write down any dreams or premonitions that come to you. Even if these thoughts and images don't make sense in the moment, they will over time, especially if you're recording the dates and the times. If something you documented connects later, you'll be able to see the correlation between when you got the information and when it manifested allowing you to see the timeline of your premonitions to manifestations.

Can you build your psychic senses? Absolutely! They are like physical muscles, not too different from going to the gym. We build our physical body and we can also build our psychic body. In later chapters, we will discuss further *how* build those "clair" muscles of yours!

Additionally, we will also discuss ways you can receive information through your various clairs. Clair means "clear" in French. However, in regard to your senses, clear is referencing the information to be without prejudice. Being a clear channel. Some clairs may be stronger for you than others, but we're also going to talk about how you can develop your weakest clair because you will only be as strong as your weakest link.

A psychic connection requires a higher vibration than being grounded in the physical world. In part, it's like the channel to a radio station. You need to change the channel to tune into the psychic frequency. As a result, your first step is to raise your vibration before creating a soul-to-soul connection. Imagine a cord running from your heart to your recipient's heart. This is how the psychic connection works. After raising your vibration and expanding your aura upwards and forwards, you create an energy link with your higher self and the aura of your sitter.

When we tune into the soul of a sitter, we can see if there is an overall purpose. What is their soul craving? What do they wish they had time for or what is something new they want to try? Are they holding themselves back? If so, where? When you do a psychic reading, you can go into areas of their life. You can tune into love and relationship. Are they married or single? Are they craving love? Are they lonely? Do they want children? If that relationship is coming forward, what is the timing?

How about career? Are they doing what they love? Are they happy with what they are doing, or do they desire something more? Are they satisfied? Are they staying in a job solely for financial reasons? Is there a greater calling for them? Is there another avenue they should be? Are they due for a raise or a different position or title? Are they moving companies? Relocating? There are so many potential questions someone can have around their career.

Now let's talk finances. We all want to know about the money honey. So, what *is* going on with money? Is more money coming in the near future? Are they struggling with money? Is money a block for them? What are the blocks that your sitter is experiencing?

Legal may also be a concern. Is there a pending lawsuit? Are they buying a new car or are they purchasing a house? What is coming up with contracts for them in their life?

Another area to consider is health. Now this one we always have to be a little more careful about because we can't go around diagnosing our clients. Stating a disclaimer before you begin is extremely important. Before diving into health, a simple "I am not a doctor and I cannot diagnose, but if you're open to hearing what I'm receiving, I'll be more than happy to share it with you".

Creating a strong link will help the information you receive come from pure source and not your personal beliefs or projections. This is essential when sitting for another. You would not want your own standards and opinions to impact a recipient's reading.

An honor system is essential to your work. It is irresponsible to use your gift to make decisions for other people. You want your psychic connection to be of the highest good and one of integrity. Remind your sitter that they have free will. Telling them they are the captain of their ship and that they already have all of the answers, reminds them that they are accountable for their own life and decisions.

Let them know that they have *FREE WILL*, allowing them to change their course as needed.

CHAPTER 3 |
WHAT IS A MEDIUMSHIP?

*An individual held to be a channel of communication
between the earthly world and a world of spirits*
—Merriam Webster Dictionary

Mediumship is the ability for the soul of someone in
the physical world to connect and communicate
with the soul of someone in the spirit world. Death
is merely the transition and dissolution of the
physical body. The soul itself transcends death.

The soul lives on and resides on what is considered
the other side of the veil. What is the veil? The veil
is like an imaginary translucent curtain where Spirit
is just on the other side. If you expand your aura
outwards and with a slight upwards intention, you
can feel the spirit world. However, it should be
noted that this veil is not as far away as some may

17

believe, but in close proximity to the physical world. Although most people don't *see* this "realm" with their physical eye, it's very clear that it exists.

When someone connects and communicates with spirit, they may use their clair senses. These clairs are heightened senses (extra sensory perception, esp.). This may allow a person to see spirit (with either the physical eye or inner eye). Perhaps they hear spirit (with the physical ear or inner ear). Some feel spirit around them or they may simply know spirit is among them.

Spirit wants to communicate with those in the living and show us that they are still very much among us and around us. The ability and gift that someone has to connect with the spirit world is what we refer to as mediumship.

CHAPTER 4 |
SPIRIT GUIDES 101

What are spirit guides?

Spirit guides are souls on the other side that have either been assigned or have volunteered to help a person in the physical realm. There are several types of guides.

Ascended Masters
Ascended Masters are super charged spiritual beings. They once walked a spiritual path on earth but have now transcended to the point of no longer needing to reincarnate to the earth plane to learn karmic lessons. Ascended Masters still have a purpose to teach, heal and become spiritual guides to many. They are represented as gods, saints and religious and spiritual symbols we honor today in

art, sculpture, scripture, music, and more. Some examples of known Ascended Masters are Jesus Christ, Buddha, Mother Theresa, Saint Germain, Krishna, just to name a few.

Master Guides

Master Guides are assigned to you at birth. When you come into the physical world your master guide is already there with you. You may not have met your master guide in either this physical world or in a past life. They are generally not your relative but have had enough experience to help and guide you on your life's journey. They still reincarnate yet they are old souls and their main purpose is to guide you on your life's lesson and offer guidance as you embark on your spiritual path.

Task Guides

Other guides are more like *task guides*. They are assigned for a specific reason. A *task guide* steps in around a particular area or during a specific time in your life when you may need more specialized assistance. They sometimes step in around a particular impending decision. For example, what career is best for you? What is your purpose? They may show up when you're switching careers or when there's a major transition. Perhaps you're having a medical issue, therefore a guide will step in that specializes in that to help with an illness, diagnosis or to find the best treatment. They may simply step in to offer you support in a time of need.

Maybe you are inventing or creating something. There may be a special guide that steps in for that. For these task guides, they move on once their assignment is complete.

Gatekeeper

Then there is the *gatekeeper*. You can think of them as the bouncer at the night club. The gatekeeper is the threshold to allowing certain spirits to step through and communicate with you and which spirits are forbidden access. If you set an intention with your gatekeeper to only allow the highest vibrational spirits to step through, your gatekeeper will honor those intentions. This allows them to discern "who gets through" to communicate with you.

Family Members

Your loved ones may also be on the other side guiding you. They may be there to support you or to help you open up your medium gifts. Grandparents, Aunts, Uncles, Friends, Parents, Siblings, etc. There are no limits as to who on the other say may step forward to offer love and support. They may be there to remind you of your hidden talents or to remind you of *who* you are and from *where* you came. Some of your family guides may be either generational or karmic. They may even be family members that go back several generations and are with you to help clear karmic links in this lifetime.

Having a connection and a relationship with your guides is a very important part of your spiritual growth. If you build a connection with your guides you can communicate with them more clearly and effectively. You will find that your guides will help to direct you, inspire you, and help you to stay on track.

The relationship you build with your guides provides you with the resources to lean on your spirit tribe. Your spirit tribe always has your back.

Some people get very discouraged when they don't know the names of their guides or they don't see them. Release the need to have names and expectations when you are starting out. It's more about trusting that your guides are there and believing, trusting and surrendering to the power of the guides. Whether you feel that it's your imagination or not, through the practice of meditation and raising your vibration you will begin to experience these guides around you. Be patient as it does take practice and commitment. You want to develop the ability to blend with those guides so that you're not pushing or trying too hard to make that connection. If you push, you will simply lock into your logical mind which results in naturally lowering your vibration.

When you allow yourself to relax with your guides, you may begin to receive more information. For example, your guides may give you their name using a symbol or object. Let's say you see a word or image on a billboard. In that moment, if a thought or feeling pops in "oh, that's the name" or "this is a message", this is when trusting it is most important.

It is about knowing that there is someone there helping you make life choices guiding you when you are feeling lost, concerned or feeling stressed. They serve as a reminder that you don't have to keep it all to yourself and that you do have someone to connect and communicate with that wants to see you succeed.

Honorable Mention: Angels

Angels are different than other guides but deserve recognition. Angels have never incarnated into the physical world and come in with unconditional love to offer support, protection and to watch over us. Guardian angels are assigned to help to keep you safe.

EXERCISES

EXERCISE #1
Connecting with a Guide

This is an exercise to connect with ANY of your guides. Simply allow whomever chooses to help you with this exercise to step in. Sit in a quiet space and do a 20-minute meditation with the purpose of connecting any one of your (spirit) guides. See if you can connect to who they are, what their personality is like, what was their life like in the physical if they had one, how do they serve you and write down any messages they are giving you. Ask your guide to give you a sign for you to look for in the physical realm. Surrender to the process and do not create expectations. What sign and the message you received?

EXERCISE #2
Guided Meditation

Listen to a guided meditation for the purposes of connecting to a loved one in spirit. Allow the meditation to unveil how a loved one is helping you from the other side. What are they showing you? Are they guiding you? This guided meditation can be supplemented for

One has been created by the author for purchase for a nominal fee:
https://rebelations.mykajabi.com/offers/JxjJoLuu

CHAPTER 5 |
RAISING YOUR VIBRATION

Why do we need to raise our vibration? In order to connect to the higher self and soul of the sitter, we must first raise our own vibration. Raising our vibration allows us to connect to our own soul and the soul of the sitter. When we connect to the higher self we are seeing, feeling, hearing and knowing what is of the highest good for our client. We always want to begin a session or connection from the place of high vibration. That vibrational connection is essential to a strong link. Otherwise, we would only be delivering information from our ego space, not our soul space. The ego is a place we wouldn't want to do a reading from as we only want to work for the highest self and soul so that we are tuning into what is all-knowing.

Learning how to raise your vibration takes time and practice. Through diligence you will learn how to click into the frequency of your higher self with ease. Initially, you may not realize whether or not you are in a higher vibration. Becoming more aware and sensitive to your own mind, body and soul will help you to sense the different vibrations within your own self. Meditation and breath control are key components to tuning into raising your vibration. You will have to practice both of these to build your endurance in holding a higher vibration for a longer period of time. Be patient with yourself as it may take time to build your love of both.

How do you raise your vibration? There are several ways you can raise your vibration.

Here are a few exercises to help you raise your vibration. Feel free to try these on your own.

1. GLOW BALLOON:

Sit in a comfortable position. This can be in a chair, on a couch or even sitting on the floor. Your feet may be placed firmly on the ground or folded beneath you. You may even wish to lay flat on your back for meditation. Use whatever position works best for you. There is NO right or wrong.

Now, close your eyes and take a deep breath. Inhale slowly through your nose and exhale slowly through your mouth. Take a few deep breaths and with each breath you release the worries of the day. Allow your body to feel still without the need to fidget.

As you inhale, imagine yourself as a pure white balloon. With each breath the balloon rises higher and higher into the sky. As you inhale in, you begin to feel yourself getting lighter and lighter. Soon you are floating. Now imagine your feet are leaving the ground.

Each breath, lighter and lighter.

As you rise up you are now outside of any building you may have been in. You are now looking down on the building. You are not scared. You know you are safe. You continue to use your breath until you are in the sky with the clouds. You may even notice shapes within the clouds. You are completely surrendered in this beautiful glow space. This is a space of love. This is the point in which you realize your vibration is exactly where it needs to be for you to connect.

Enjoy this space.

In this space you may meditate, release, indulge or simply be. Take note of how this vibration feels within your own body.

When you are ready, gently allow yourself to use your breath and in reverse, lowering yourself back into your physical body. Using breath, feel the vibration getting lower and lower. Feel it go back into your head. With each breath, lower and lower. Now feel that vibration go down your neck and your arms. Feel the vibration go out the palms of your hands and through the tips of your fingers. Lower and lower. Now feel the vibration go down your hips and begin to move them around. The vibration will now go through your legs, knees and push the vibration out through the bottom of the soles of your feet back into the center of the earth. Be sure to wiggle your toes in your shoes or on the ground upon finishing this exercise to help you ground back into the physical realm.

2. IN THE POWER

In the power is exactly as it sounds. POWERFUL. This is an exercise in which you allow yourself to sit still in a comfortable position. Allow your breath to slow down and use it to center yourself. In the power is a time in which you connect to your soul and the infinite power it already possesses. You use this time to be 100% completely within your own soul. You remember your infinite love and power. You do not escape to thoughts of the day or chores. You forgo your desire to check your social media and give yourself permission to ignore all distractions. In this time is when you pull all of your outside fragmented energy within your being. You sit in your full power. This is a great exercise to use to not only remember your greatness, but to raise your vibration. What makes sitting in the power different from meditating? Sitting in the power is about being fully connected and immersed in your soul's gift and potential. You are connecting to your soul and remembering who you are and your soul imprint. Meditating is about putting an intention or thought out there and then connecting to that thought and intention through technique. For instance, you may meditate to connect with your guides or find clarity regarding a situation. Perhaps you are meditating to raise your vibration or train your body and mind to embrace stillness.

Sitting in the power can become part of your daily routine. Again, this may take practice for you to feel accustom to your own power. We become disassociated with our own power, so the intention of this exercise is to reunite you with your own soul power.

3. AURA EXPANSION:

A third exercise that can raise vibration is to expand your aura. We all have an aura. An aura is the energetic field that surrounds your physical body. Since the aura is energy, we can move it and expand it. We can shift our aura upwards, outwards, and forwards. To raise your vibration, simply imagine pushing your aura upwards and outwards. Pushing it to expand as big as it will go! Again, breath is extremely helpful with this exercise. With each breath in you build your power. With each exhale, you use that power to push the aura and expand it. Imagine you are blowing up a balloon. With each exhale the balloon gets larger. This is like your aura. Expanding your aura as far as it will go will help you to raise your vibration.

4. OTHER OPTIONS

Other ways to raise your vibration are through dance, movement, breath and laughter. Movement is energy. Even a simple smile can raise your vibration! Sprinkle these into your daily routine to elevate your mood and vibration!

PART 2

Essentials

CHAPTER 6 |
GROUNDING & GRATITUDE

Grounding and gratitude are two vital aspects of developing your gifts. The purpose of grounding is to reconnect to the earth's energy. Grounding helps you quiet your mind chatter, ease anxiety and allows you to feel more present in your physical body. When you are *not* grounded you will feel aloof, spacey and disoriented. You may experience poor sleep or find yourself easily distracted, difficulty focusing and possibly even a sense of paranoia. Focusing too much on material objects, engaging with social media constantly or being overly-concerned with what others think of you is also a sign of being ungrounded. This doesn't mean you shouldn't care about yourself or take care of yourself in a healthy way. This is more in reference to being so overly self-conscious of what others think of you that you are unable to feel secure. Being grounded is an energetic balance between your mind, body and spirit as it relates to the earth's energy. When you are grounded you feel more centered and in return, creating a pure channel for spirit to utilize because your mind chatter is at bay. The monkey mind interrupts your connection, so you want to learn how to put it off to the side during any connection.

There are several ways in which you can practice grounding and it's imperative that you take the time and effort to do it before attempting any links. Being ungrounded feels like a spirit hangover. You feel dizzy, emotional, negative thoughts churn in your head, and you become volatile because you are susceptible to the impact of the energy in your environment. This creates an unstable energetic fluctuation resulting in emotional highs and lows. You will be an energetic pinball machine being flung into bumpers and at the mercy of the flippers. Your thoughts will be scattered, and you may experience confusion and lack of clarity. Reconnecting to the earth's energy allows you to feel stable and strong. Additionally, it helps with your boundaries and provides an energetic shield against negative outside energy.

Grounding vs. Lowering Vibration

Some students confuse grounding with lowering vibration. Grounding is **not** the act of lowering your vibration, but rather merging and balancing your energetic frequency to be in complete and total alignment. On the other hand, lowering your vibration is like turning the vibration dial down. Imagine lowering the volume on the radio. You turn the dial left and the volume decreases. It gets softer until you can no longer hear it. By lowering your vibration, you are consciously letting the vibration move down the chambers back to the physical body, space and time. Imagine pulling the string of a balloon and that balloon goes from once dancing in the sky to receding back into the holder's hand.

When you are grounded and centered you are in a space of presentness. Being present allows you to be in the here and now at this exact moment of existence. It is in this space that your creativity is maximized since you are not distracted by thoughts initiated by the ego. With presentness you are allowing your body to be one with this exact moment in time. This connection frees your creative mind to make that link to the spirit world. Presentness is critical to your overall well-being and being of service to spirit. Integrating presentness into your day to day practice will help you feel better energetically and allow you the opportunity to focus on your creativity so inspiration can step forward.

Gratitude also plays an important role in maintaining a strong connection. If you take your gift for granted and you assume it will always be there without any effort or commitment on your part or if you lack respect for it, it will cease to exist. If you use your connection for ill will, it will shut down at some point. Spirit will not work with the egocentric person. It is a privilege and honor to serve spirit and staying humble and grateful in that recognition will help you to sustain that relationship with spirit. This is why grounding and gratitude are essential elements to your overall development. Let's discuss how you can exercise both.

Grounding Exercises:

1. Visualization

Allow yourself to sit comfortably as you slip into a light meditation. Slow your breath inhaling through your nose and exhaling through your mouth. Do this a few times slowly until you begin to feel your heart rate decrease and your body relax. Next, imagine a gold chord extending from your root chakra into the center of the earth. This chord anchors you to Mother Earth and reminds you that you are one with the universe. You feel the energy from the earth's core rise up and envelope you with love. This exercise can be done approximately 5-10 minutes prior to any connection. If you need longer, feel free to take as much time as you need. As you progress with your practice, getting grounded will become easier for you.

2. Toe Wiggle

An excellent way to ground yourself is to wiggle your toes in your shoes or directly to the floor. By wiggling your toes, you are reigniting your earth energy. You will feel an immediate shift in your body. You may even choose to walk barefoot in the grass. Letting the soles of your feet immerse themselves in the blades of the grass will trigger your natural connection to the earth.

3. Food

It's known that certain foods have a reputation for being conducive to grounding. Depending on your particular dietary needs you may need to adjust accordingly and modify as needed to meet your specific requirements.

Meat

Meat has a reputation for grounding due to its high protein contents. The more protein it has the more it will affect your grounding. For example, per *Men's Health* magazine lean red meat has the most protein with 36g of protein per 100g. Chicken follows second with 33g per 100g. Lamb contains 25g per 100g and cod has 18g per 100g. How many times have you finished a class, connection or meditation and then craved a hamburger? This is your body's natural yearn for grounding. *Please note that although meat can be grounding, it can also lower vibration.*

Some feel that they are naturally clearer without eating meat, so this becomes a personal preference.

Alternatives

If you are a vegan or vegetarian, then you would modify the intake to supplement other alternatives such as Soy Protein Isolate which contains 88g per 100g or Tofu coming in at 17g per 100g.

Root Vegetables

Other options include root vegetables. Vegetables grown from the soil carry energy. This energy is then transferred to you upon consumption. Root vegetable will help you feel more anchored to the earth but won't dim your intuitive light. Some root vegetables include *carrots, potatoes, onions, beets, turnips, peanuts,* etc. Watch for allergies and other known responses to your intake.

Chocolate

Chocolate comes cacao beans and are a delicious treat for grounding. For best results, choose chocolate this is natural, unsweetened and higher in cacao percentage. It may not taste as sweet as your regular candy bar, but avoiding the false sugars and fillers is better for your body.

4. I am GROOT

You may not be the infectious character from the Marvel comic books, but if you think like Groot, you may just become more grounded. Start with visualizing yourself as a tree. A grand old tree where you allow your legs to go as deep into the earth as the oldest tree roots. Another option is to find a tree and give it the biggest hug you can. Both of these will help you in grounding and connecting to the earth's energy.

5. Crystals

Crystals offer extraordinary elements to assist with grounding. Since they are naturally derived from the earth, they exude a powerful energy to help you with grounding.

Hematite Stone is an excellent resource for grounding. With its intense magnetic energy and subtle vibrational nuances, you will feel a pull with this stone. It helps to eliminate imbalance, negative thoughts and pulls negative energy away from your being.

Other stones beneficial for grounding include: Black Tourmaline, Smoky Quartz, Red Jasper and Shungite.

6. Spring Cleaning

Grab a broom and start sweeping! There is something about cleaning that serves as a natural conduit to grounding. Removing the toxins and negative energy from surfaces and air mixed with the physical act of cleaning offer up a wonderful method to not only ground but keep a clean house!

Gratitude Exercises

Exercise 1

Each morning before getting out of bed, spend 5 minutes listing 5 things you are grateful for in your life and why they are important to you. Be specific and go deeper with your gratitude list. This will help you to feel more abundant each and every day.

Exercise 2

Try an act of thoughtfulness this week. Surprise someone with a token of your appreciation. This can be a small gesture. Like letting someone leave an hour early on Friday and they still get paid. Or buying a lunch or anything at all that just shows appreciation.

CHAPTER 7|
RECEIVING INFORMATION

So how does a psychic or medium receive their information? They may receive it in a variety of ways. The primary tools that a psychic utilizes in their connection are known as clairs. Clairs are the "clear" senses of your seeing, feeling, hearing, knowing, tasting and smelling. Although most people have these basic senses, when there is a psychic connection they are heightened. They are more in tune than the average person. This "clear" sense becomes your clair.

If you hear a psychic talk about their "clairs", they are referring to the senses being used within their connection. These senses may be within your imagination (mind's eye) or in an outside physical sense (outside).

For example, when you see with your physical eyes, this is your eyesight at work. However, when a message or premonition is given through your eyesight this is your clairvoyance. It's your "clear" seeing. This flash of an image may be for something in the future (a premonition) or it may be a signal that someone is trying to communicate with you. Regardless, if a picture pops into your imagination or your eye is drawn to something in the physical that lingers and connects to a message or premonition, that that is your *clairvoyance* at work.

If you *hear* a voice or sound (whether it be inside your imagination or with your physical hearing), that is your *clairaudience* and when you experience a *feeling* that is your *clairsentience*. If a *smell* comes in that is *clairscent* and the use of *taste* is *clairgustance*. For example, you may either *smell* coffee or *taste* coffee.

In summary, seeing is *clairvoyance*, hearing is *clairaudience*, feeling is *clairsentience* and thoughts popping in that feel like facts, they are known as *claircognizance*. Taste is *clairgustance* and smell is *clairscent*!

When you actively develop all of your clair senses you are expanding your potential as to what is available for you to pull from within your resources. Let's dive deeper into the various clairs.

CHAPTER 8 |
DIVING DEEPER INTO CLAIRS

In both a mediumship and psychic connection, your clairs are your tools. These tools are essentially the same. The tools will help you receive the information. It's the *source* of the tool that makes a distinction between psychic and medium.

For instance, if the tool is coming directly from a loved one in spirit (*for example, your loved one gives you an image directly*) This would be considered mediumship. Contrarily, if that same image is coming from your higher self-or the soul of your sitter, this is a psychic connection. This is why it's important to build the tools so that you have them in your toolbox for BOTH psychic and mediumistic connections.

Let's discuss the various tools available to you. The clairs are essentially your hammer, saw, drill and screwdriver that are there to help you build a strong psychic or medium foundation for a powerful connection.

Building your clairs is as important to your psychic and medium connection as weight training is to a body builder. In order to have a strong and balanced body, you must incorporate exercises that force each muscle group to grow. For example, a shapely arm needs the bicep, tricep and shoulder developed to create overall balance. If you only focus on one, you may end up looking like Popeye with outrageously developed forearms but no bicep or triceps to balance it out!

So, in order to build your balanced connection with spirit, commit to developing all of your clairs. Some may be more natural for you, but it's absolutely possible to strengthen each of them individually and conjointly.

REMEMBER! You are only as strong as your weakest clair!

CLAIRCOGNIZANCE:

This is your sense of "clear knowing". Without any prompting, you will have a thought pop into your head and just KNOW it to be true. It's almost as if a thought will magically appear within your mind and you know it's a fact without questioning it. This is the claircognizance at work for you. Claircognizance is one of the most popular clairs and its how many people discover they have something different about them. You will think of someone and then the phone rings and it's them on the other end! You will see someone and just know the mood they are in at that moment.

CLAIRVOYANCE:

Clairvoyance is your sense of seeing. This may be through your physical eye or your inner eye. The inner eye will seem like it's just your imagination at work. Clairvoyance may also draw your attention to something in the physical. It may be a billboard, traffic light, perhaps it's something in nature. Anything that pulls your eye and holds it there for an extra second or beat is usually a clairvoyant sign for you to notice. If it's followed by a thought of a loved in one in that moment, then that loved one is sending you a message! If the loved one is in the living, they are thinking of you and this is a psychic message. If that loved one is in spirit, they are letting you know that they are with you in that specific moment and this is a medium connection.

For clairvoyance, there are many ways to perceive the information given. You may be shown an image or a video. For some, they have said it feels like they are watching a movie. Others see this movie in color while some only see in black and white. There are those that tend to see just one image without anything connected to it. All of this is usually within the mind's eye. This is your third eye as it's frequently referred to within the field. When someone is saying to "open your third eye chakra" they are essentially encouraging you to allow your clairvoyance to open.

It would be easy to just wave a magic wand and "Who La!" your third eye is now open, but it may also take discipline and practice for it to open completely. In a later chapter you will be provided with exercises that are specifically designed to help you open your clairvoyance or "clear seeing" more easily.

By opening your third eye or clairvoyance, you will be able to see images sent to you either by spirit or the soul of your sitter to help decipher the messages more clearly. Images may be that of a physical description, sign, symbol or even a name or number may display in the form of an image.

CLAIRAUDIENCE:

Clairaudience is your "clear hearing". This is where you may hear with your physical ear or within your inner ear. The inner ear clairaudience will also feel as if it's within your own imagination.

You may hear your name called, voices that sound as if they are others or your own, music, knocking, etc. There are many reasons why each of the above happen to you. It may be your guides trying to get your attention or it could be spirit talking to you directly. Perhaps, it's a spirit for someone else who is trying to get your attention to deliver a message on their behalf.

For your physical clairaudience, this will come through in the form of music. Have you ever thought of a loved one in spirit and then your favorite song came on the radio? It's the song that floods you with memories of them and you feel them around you. This is no coincidence. This is your loved one using clairaudience to get your attention.

Clairaudience can also be a physical noise that you hear. Perhaps it's a horn, alarm, siren, etc. Spirit will use sounds to send you messages in the same way they will pull your attention to an image in the physical world. Spirit has the intelligence to use whatever means possible to get you to notice them. In general, since we spend so much time dismissing what we are receiving, spirit is forced to work overtime and in very creative ways to get us to "look, hear, see and feel". Once you start paying attention by expanding your awareness, their ability to communicate in as many ways as possible becomes endless.

CLAIRSENTIENCE:

Clairsentience is the tool of feeling. It may start out in an empathetic way. Clairsentience can be used for blending with the spirit world. By using your "clear feeling" you will receive impressions. For example, you may receive the impression of a chest tightening as you connect to a spirit. This may be their way of letting you know that they passed from a condition or issue in the chest area.

Your clear sense of feeling or clairsentience is extremely helpful in terms of tuning into your sitter to see what their soul may be able to handle during a sitting. Many psychics and mediums forget the importance of remembering to tune into the client to see how much information they are able to handle at this time. *What can their soul handle?* There is a responsibility to uphold the highest ethics and standards if you are to do this work on a professional level. When your clairsentience is strong, it provides an opportunity to bring that spirit connection in closer to you. Through blending with the spirit, you will feel certain characteristics. For instance, how they walked. Did they have a limp? Did they need assistance? Were they able to walk at all? Were they bedridden? All of these questions and more can be answered using your clairsentience. They may give you a sense of their mannerisms or personality. Rather than hearing a word or seeing a picture, clairsentience is a specific impression based on feeling.

On a psychic level, your sitter may have questions around direction, opportunities or a specific outcome. Your clairsentience and compass can help provide a yes or no to their questions.

Now that we've gone over the various clairs, it's time to dive into the exercises that will help *you* strengthen these clairs. Remember, by building your clairs, you will be building a stronger connection with both your psychic and medium gifts. We will now discuss one of the most important tools to your development. *The Compass*.

CHAPTER 9 |
THE COMPASS

Although the compass is a simple tool, it is perhaps your most important one. It will literally help you dive in with greater detail to any question you pose to spirit and the universe by providing you with an easy yes or no answer. The compass is similar to a pendulum except the compass resides WITHIN you! The compass is based on your clairsentience.

Here's how it works. Imagine a circle that is just above your belly button and just below your rib cage. This is where your intuition lies. Your gut feeling is also derived from this area as well. Place the palm of your hand inside this circle. Next, imagine a vertical line that goes directly down the center of the circle. The compass will tilt to one side for YES and the opposite side for NO.

To establish which is your YES side and which is your NO side, you will use your clairsentience. Let's start by establishing your YES side. I want you to state a **FACT**. This is **not** something you must ponder or even give a second thought to as you already know this to be true. *The statement should be simple*. A compound sentence will not work as effectively. For instance, you may want to say, "My first name is XXX". Now, tune in to *FEEL*, which side your compass tilted. Did it naturally tilt to your left or did it naturally to your right? Whichever side it tilted to will be your **YES** side. There is no right or wrong, as either side is simply how spirit wants to work with you. Now that you established your YES side, it's time to determine your NO side. This is usually the opposite side, but it's always good to validate it by stating a **LIE**. Make an absolute false statement. The compass should naturally tile the opposite way.

It may not feel incredibly strong the first time you do this exercise, but it's about building the spirit muscle. With time, practice and consistency you will see how effective the compass will be in providing you with simple yes or no answers by simply using your clairsentience.

You may be wondering what kind of questions your compass can help you with during a connection. Here's a few ways that your compass can provide deeper levels of detail.

Imagine you have a man in spirit, and he has stated he is the grandfather on the father's side of your sitter. This is your clairaudience that you "heard" him provide the relationship. He now shows you a watch. Your clairvoyance has now been sparked as you were shown an image in your mind's eye. Suppose you want to know about the watch. Rather than wait for the spirit to "drip" the information down to you, which leads to pauses, lack of connection and confusion, you can ask him direct questions using your compass to receive the answers via your clairsentience.

Was that your watch?
(Your compass tilts to your YES side)

Did you give that watch to your sitter?
(You compass tilts to your NO side)

Would your son have this watch?
(compass says YES)

Is this watch supposed to be given to your grandson here? *(compass gives you a YES)*

Is there an inscription on the back of the watch
(compass gives you a yes)

At this point, you may want to try and pull in a clairvoyant image of the inscription or ask the spirit what the inscription says to receive the information clairaudiently.

You see *"love above all"*

Now, let's see how this compass is delivered in a practical way during a medium reading.

"I have man here who is letting me know that he is your grandfather on your father's side. Would you understand this?"

Sitter: *"Yes"*

Medium: *"He is showing me his watch. You remember that he wore a watch, is that correct?"*

Sitter: Yes

Medium: *"Your grandfather indicates that this watch was given to your father. Would you know that to be true?"*

Sitter: *"Yes, I do."*

Medium: *"Well, your grandfather has just indicated that he hopes the watch is to be given to you one day."*

Sitter: *"Oh, yes, my father mentioned that it was going to be passed down to me one day!"*

Medium: *"He also shows me an image of an inscription that shows the word "love above all". Do you know the inscription on the watch?"*

Sitter: Oh, I believe that *is* the inscription!

Medium: *"Check with your father on the inscription, but this is what he is showing me, and I know that your grandfather "loves you above all".*

The compass will work in much the same way during a psychic session. Perhaps the sitter would like to know if they are getting that new position that they just interviewed for last week. Does the compass say *YES* or *NO*? Will I have another child? *YES* or *NO*? Will my significant other ever propose to me? *YES* or *NO*?

To take it a step further, your compass is a fabulous way to help **YOU** in your own decision-making. Should you ask for a raise? Take on that new

64

project? Travel this year? Buy that new car? Move residences? Trust that friend? Rather than getting lost in the conscious mind, you can allow your compass to utilize your clairsentience to help you hone in to provide you with clarity regarding your own decisions.

Exercise

Spend a full day exercising your compass muscle. Go to work and flex your compass throughout the day. Try it as many times as you can as you are going about your day. See how many times your compass was *"right on"*. Practice this multiple days and times. When you begin to feel more confident, try it with a friend!

CHAPTER 10 |
EMPATHS AND MORE

An empath is someone who can feel the feelings or emotions of another. The feelings may come through so strongly that you may interpret those feelings as your own when in fact, they are those of another.

One way for an empath to discern if the feeling is relevant to them or not is to ask the simple question "is this my own feeling or that of another". By being in tune, you will feel the difference and know whether that emotion is connected to you or someone else. When it is for another, simply release it with a positive intention of love and light.

Empaths can sometimes struggle with "energy vampires". You all know that person. The one who makes you feel more exhausted after a conversation with them! The one who is all about ME! ME! ME! Well, they have a name! *Energy Vampire*! An energy vampire is someone who feels the whole world revolves around them! They seem to complain about EVERYTHING. They gossip, tend to be poor listeners and leave you feeling stressed, anxious and overwhelmed.

You may work with them, be related to them or even in a relationship with them! I hate to say it, but you may have even given BIRTH to them! Your nurturing nature may make it difficult for you to set boundaries. You may feel a desire to "fix" them or "love them enough", however, energy vampires are not usually open to change.

What do you do? Do you have to deal with this draining person for the rest of your life? Honestly, the answer could be yes. But you also have the ability to make some changes so that this person's energy doesn't feel as intense.

It would be unrealistic to tell you that you can disconnect from every single energy vampire you come in contact with. *Energy Vampires* run rampant in our world! Whether its social media or the workplace, you probably encounter an *energy vampire* every day!

Here are THREE exercises to help you handle *Energy Vampires*.

1. Turn your mirrors out

Normally, we take energy from others in. If you're an empath (meaning you feel the emotions of another being) than you are even more sensitive to the impact of energy vampires. Absorbing this energy over and over may leave you feeling exhausted, depressed and overwhelmed. *Energy Vampires* are draining your battery. If you turn your mirrors out (meaning you reverse the energy flow) they are forced to look at their own energy. You can simply do this by thinking of your palms as mirrors. Remember the "talk to the hand" that was so popular a few years ago? Yes, think of it somewhat like that. You basically reject the energy the other person is exuding. Doing this will really help you own what is your energy and give back what is not.

2. Clear Protection Box

This exercise is credited to the great Lisa Williams and its incredibly effective. Think of a clear telephone booth. It's solid, stable and protective. You get inside (energetically). You can emit your energy without sacrificing your power, yet someone else's energy cannot penetrate the box. This is your protective haven! This will work great in crowds, workplaces and malls, places where the energy can be so heavy you leave feeling like you're coming down with a cold! The clear protection box takes practice. You have to build up the wall energetically so don't worry if takes you some time to build up the ability to maintain it for a period of time.

3. Clearing Tools

There are many tools that can be used in helping you cleanse the energy left behind by an energy vampire. Although, cleansing can be done with intention, some people may find the use of tools to make it easier and concrete. Sage is a great source for burning and clearing energy in a house or space that feels a bit heavy. Another great tool is carrying the crystal Black Tourmaline. It's known for its protective elements and can be placed by a work station, in a pocket or a purse. Black Tourmaline can definitely be helpful against the ever-enduring battle against the energy vampire! Pine Sol is an excellent clearing tool. Give your space a good scrub with it and you'll immediately feel the shift in the energy of your domain.

Establishing boundaries within your relationships is imperative to being a strong light worker. Upholding boundaries doesn't mean you can't continue to give, nurture and nourish those around you. It simply means that you begin to discern *when*, *where* and *how* you *choose* to distribute your energy so that you aren't running so low energetically that you are left with nothing more to give. Don't be afraid to refrain from continuing relationships if there is an imbalance in energy exchange. You have to know your limits and uphold them. By implementing boundaries in your life, you will be creating balance which is essential to your overall well-being. In Chapter 24 we focus on boundaries.

CHAPTER 11 |
EXPANDING YOUR AWARENESS

Another important aspect of a psychic and medium connection is expanding your awareness. Expanding your awareness is a great way to develop your psychic gifts as it helps you to pick up on subtleties throughout your connection. When your awareness is expanded, the details become stronger and more vivid within your readings. So *how* do you expand our awareness?

Firstly, review and practice the exercises previously mentioned. Practice is *key*. Other suggestions include isolating your senses as much as possible to hone in on developing them individually. When a sense, such as your sight, hearing, thoughts or feelings are isolated, you will strengthen them since you won't be using the other senses as a crutch to lean on. You would be surprised at how many times

73

you intertwine your senses throughout your daily routine without even thinking about it. In most cases this will be a valuable asset so that you can tell the story of what you are receiving more accurately, but for the purposes of development, you will want each clair to be able to "stand on its own".

Meditation is a wonderful tool to focus on expanding your awareness. For some, meditation may seem a tedious task. You may find yourself preferring to empty the dishwasher, scrub the bathroom floor or mindlessly scan social media. *Self-discipline* is needed to avoid these distractions. When you focus on the practice of being comfortable with yourself, higher-self and spirit guides, you will find that your clairs will expand beyond your imagination.

Meditation is so imperative to our own growth. In addition to helping you expand your awareness; it will help with grounding yourself. This is key to linking a psychic connection. We have to learn how to anchor our physical body to allow an open and fluid connection.

If you are in the beginning phases of meditation, try a guided meditation. A guided meditation is a meditation that is spoken by another. They will walk you through the meditation, thus helping you visualize the intention.

At first your thoughts are going to get in the way. This is completely NORMAL. Once you learn how to quiet your "monkey mind" you will begin to settle into the meditation. Over time and with practice, you will even feel less anxious and nervous. Additionally, meditation helps you to expand and connect to different realms and energy levels. Beyond meditation, finding the peace in stillness is extremely beneficial to being able to easily tap into your higher consciousness. Practice meditation, stillness, and sitting in the power and you will begin to connect to your higher self with ease and fluidity. If you are one that has difficulty in focusing, try prioritizing your desire to develop your psychic senses. Whenever you feel disconnected from your higher self or spirit, know that meditation can help reconnect that link. Usually, the disconnect happens when you are stressed or avoiding or simply not making the time for it.

In the beginning, just do it for a few minutes at a time and then slowly add a few minutes here and there. Build your spiritual endurance and you'll find you may even enjoy your mini meditation getaways!

Exercise

Take 1 day and allow yourself to move *SLOWER*. Slow down this ONE day. Take in the sights and sounds around you. Make it a point to not move as your normal rapid pace. Take it all in. *What did you notice changed in you as you began to move slower*?

CHAPTER 12 |
OPENING YOUR IMAGINATION

We discussed your various clairs and how they can help you understand the information you are receiving. However, your overall psychic connection derives from your imagination. The more you can expand your imagination, the greater ROI (return on investment) you will get from your clairs.

So *how* do you open your imagination? As we grow older, we forget to play. You have to get out and play!

Here are 6 ways to open your imagination and expand your creativity!

COLOR

Whether you choose to stay in the lines or create your own masterpiece, pull out a box of crayons and channel Picasso! Coloring relaxes the mind, de-stresses the body and motives the imagination and helps you to develop your clairvoyance. Any coloring book will work with this exercise. Find ways to add a bit of color back into your life!

PUZZLES

Did you put puzzles together as a child? Puzzles are an incredible tool to help you utilize your imagination. From the image on the box cover, you must then sort out the pieces to re-create that image. Not only do you feel a sense of accomplishment when completing the puzzle, but you also imagine how the pieces fit together. What images are side by side? What pieces fit where? Puzzles are a great way to connect the dots of our imagination and solve the puzzle of connection! Puzzles help to strengthen your clairvoyance and your claircognizance.

MUSIC

Music is a wonderful way to connect to your imagination. Getting lost in the rhythm not only frees your soul but can open your mind.

Music can be enjoyed in various ways:

Play

Do you play an instrument? Pull out the flute or sit with the guitar. Even a tambourine can bring your imagination to life!

Dance

Dancing is an incredible way to move energy through the body, release tension and expand the mind.

Karaoke

Go for an evening of lip-syncing to your favorite songs to stimulate your creative juices.

Sing

Whether it's in the shower or on stage, singing raises vibration and allows you to connect with your imagination.

NATURE

You can't go wrong by spending a little more time in nature. Nature has so much to offer us and yet we don't spend the time we can to marinate in that energy. Whether you choose to hike in the forest or sit by the ocean, enjoying more nature not only helps you to reconnect with your soul, but it opens up your clear channel to spirit.

SAND CASTLES

Did you ever go to the beach and build sand castles as a kid? When was the last time you sat and created with your hands? Playing in the spirit sandbox expands your imagination. It's in this facet of the brain that we connect to spirit. Whether you want to use mud, clay or sand, use your hands to build your connection to spirit.

PLAY DRESS-UP

What did you want to be as a kid? Fireman? Doctor? Astronaut? Dancer? As children, we immersed ourselves in the *make-pretend* world. We felt it and believed it. Every time we were told to *"get our head out of the clouds"* or *"stop pretending"* we started to shut that part of our psyche down. Seems like the only times we give ourselves permission to play dress-up and make-pretend are on holidays like Halloween.

Why not have a dress-up for fun? Invite your kids to play with you and let them pick the characters! Don't have kids? Try borrowing the neighbors for a bit of fun. Commit to your role and you might just see your intuition soar!

By slowing down and playing more, you will build your intuition and connection to spirit. Try some playtime and you may just realize that your senses are not only heightened, but you feel more present, relaxed and connected.

AUTOMATIC WRITING

Automatic writing is a wonderful tool to help you open up that imagination and strengthen your claircognizance. Set an intention for the session and then sit with a journal and pen. Write nonstop and see what comes out! If you find yourself overthinking, that is your logic mind stepping in. When you are playing, you will have to be careful because that logic mind will want to overpower your imagination. It will want to stop you. When it does start to overpower you, simply push it aside and allow for the natural inspiration to blossom. This natural inspiration is what will help guide and drive your psychic connection.

PART 3

Deeper Details

CHAPTER 13 |
STAGES OF A READING

Believe it or not, a connection can be broken down and delivered in stages. Let's talk about the stages of a reading. Many people don't know where to begin when they receive information because it comes in all at once or in rapid flashes. As a result, they tend to deliver the information as they are receiving it. However, if you take an opportunity to hold the information and deliver it in an organized manner you will find that you are have the ability to share the details and story of the reading with more precision and accuracy. This is the *Lock-N-Load* method ™.

When a piece of information comes in, but feels out of sync or order, you simply lock that piece until it fits into the area you are talking about and bring it forward. This method takes a great trust in your connection and spirit, but when you surrender to the method, you will see how it helps to build a beautiful story of connection with flow.

In regard to stages, there are **THREE** major stages.

The *first* stage would be what we call the *HARD FACTS*. Hard facts are information or evidence that is indisputable. From any perspective or perception, it is exactly the same.

Here are a few examples of hard facts:

- Gender (Male or Female)
- Names (Living and Deceased)
- Occupations
- Relationship (to the recipient)
- Manner of passing

The *second* stage is *SOFT FACTS*. Soft facts are things that are based on perception or can be looked at differently based on the view point of the person for whom the information is being given. Your grandfather may have felt he was a fantastic dancer, but your grandmother would disagree. Or your Uncle felt he was super funny when others would bow their heads in embarrassment at his corny jokes.

Here are some examples of *Soft Facts*:

- Hobbies
- Habits
- Idiosyncrasies
- Memories
- Personality Traits
- Mannerisms

How **you** remember something from the past may not be how your sibling remembers that exact event. You have different perceptions. Taking it a step further, how you remember it may not be how *spirit* remembers it. When perception is a factor to the information, we have embarked into Stage Two-Soft Facts.

If you are connecting to a loved one in spirit, then you would be expressing the perception from their point of view (not your sitters). In a psychic connection, you are delivering the information from your sitter's point of view.

At this point you would naturally weave through stage one (Hard Facts) and stage two (Soft Facts). Imagine an infinity symbol. You would go back and forth within the information to naturally tell the story of that spirit. Starting with a few hard facts and allowing yourself naturally to glide into stage two. Then perhaps, it reverts back to a piece of hard evidence, thus, stage one. This back and forth "dance" with the connection will constitute most of the experience of the reading.

Once stage one and two have been exhausted, you move to stage three. Stage Three is the message portion of the connection or reading. This should always be given last, even if that message has come in first. You would want to start that connection off in phase one where you provide the concrete, non-disputable evidence. This may be the gender, relationship or perhaps how they transitioned. You would naturally move to stage two, perhaps a little bit about their personality or traits. Something that would be unique to them. In these phases we are building that connection from the spirit to the sitter.

The flow should be very natural and like a dance from stage one to stage two back to stage one back to stage two. It will flow side by side. If you think of the infinity sign flowing back and forth this is really how that reading will go. You'll want to unfold it slowly allow the information to develop and expand.

STAGE THREE only makes its appearance at the very end. Once you have moved back and forth between stage one and two, you'll know you have presented all of the evidential information and its now time to deliver the message, thus moving the connection into **STAGE THREE**.

Again, even if that message comes in first (which it sometimes does) we would want to deliver that message last. The message is the grand finale and serves to be the most special part of that connection from that spirit to that sitter. It serves to be the *why* the spirit came forth. It's the cherry on top!

Here are the overall steps to a connection to help you understand the overall process of linking it all together.

Step 1: Ground Yourself

Start with a grounding exercise so you feel in alignment and balanced with the earth's energy.

Step 2: Expand Your Aura

Expand your aura and raise your vibration. This can be done by sitting in the power and allowing your aura to expand upwards and outwards as needed. Use breath and visualization to help. Remember for a psychic connection to push the aura upwards and forward and for a medium connection to expand the aura upwards and outwards past your own auric field.

Step 3: Set Your Intention

Once you have done the above 2 steps, you then want to set your intention prior to the session. Setting an intention is a critical element of the overall connection. If you are doing a psychic reading you want to set the intention to bring forward what the sitter needs to know in their life. Specifically, areas they may need clarity on or general direction in regards to their purpose. Setting the intention to only work for the highest good of the soul of the sitter.

If it is a mediumship connection, you must then remember to raise that vibration higher and expand that aura further out. Set the intention to only connect to the loved ones on the other side for the highest good and to deliver information with clarity compassion. And serving with healing messages as much as possible.

Here is a sample intention to inspire you to create a personalized intention that resonates with how you wish to serve.

"Dear Spirit, Guides and Angels,

Please allow me to connect to (recipient's name) from this world and beyond to deliver messages of healing, hope and love. May I deliver the information in a way that is clearly and easily understood by (recipient's name) and may I only work for the highest good of all. With that I surrender to you."

CHAPTER 14 |
INTERPRETING INFORMATION

A common misstep in having a strong psychic or medium connection is overinterpreting. Let's say you give a client a statement and before you know it, you are hearing a big fat "NO" from them. This can leave you feeling defeated or discouraged because you think you're wrong. Yet, the root of the "NO" may be that you delivered it improperly because you misinterpreted what you initially received. Rather than jumping to conclusions or inferring information inaccurately, simply give the details as purely as you are receiving them.

For example, you see a mother holding a red rose, rather than saying "Your mother loved red roses". Simply state what you saw in your mind's eye, "your mother is holding a red rose". Now, take it further. In your mind's eye, is she extending that rose out as to give it to someone? Is she smelling the rose? Is she putting it in a vase? Is she showing you a casket? Once you have it, you can then proceed with that new information. "She is extending that rose, she's pointing it in your direction. Would you understand having a red rose from her?"

Delivering information in this straightforward way will eliminate miscommunication. Not only is it effective in keeping your own thoughts out of the way, but it helps your recipient to receive the information in a more bite-sized and direct way. This alleviates pressure on your client to figure out what you mean or rattle their minds trying to sort out the various reasons for the rose.

Sitters will appreciate your delivery process and you will find it to increase your accuracy in readings.

If you overinterpret the information, more than likely you will receive no's from the sitter. Then naturally, you may panic and start trying to give more details and more information as you tumble into your logical mind. Try to remember that if your sitter doesn't know the first bits then giving them more will only make it more confusing. Rather than going into more details, go back to the pieces that you did deliver and then go over them again with the sitter. Give them exactly as you received them.

Think of it as a house. You are knocking on the front door with your first pieces. No one answers the door. Rather than trying to force yourself through that front door, look at the information, see how it is interpreted. Rephrase it and try a side door, the back door, a window, if needed! By breaking down what you gave, it gives you an opportunity to rebuild that link and create an opportunity for the recipient to understand the connections.

Interpreting the "hits" that come through takes practice and imagination. By expanding your imagination, more variables will come forward allowing you to then ask more questions of spirit. The more endless possibilities you create with your connection, the more spirit has to work with in giving you a yes or no around a particular piece. Spirit will pull from your reference. Think of your reference as a data bank. We want that to be as full as possible.

When a spirit gives you details, do you struggle wondering if they're referring to themselves or the sitter? One of the ways to determine is to simply ask the spirit. "Is this for you or the sitter?" See what response you get. Another way to determine is to look at the POV of the image (if given one). Let's say you are shown a necklace. Is the spirit showing you a point of view of her holding it or putting it on herself? Is she showing you an image of the sitter putting it on (as if she's looking at the sitter)? Is she holding it in her hand? Is the hand older looking, younger looking? It's about being aware of the nuances of the images, thoughts, feelings and sounds you are receiving and then tuning into the perception of that evidence to discern who it's for.

Now this is where that compass comes in handy as well. When you have an image, you can ask yes or no questions to drill down on the meaning of that image. The same holds true for all of your clairs. Whether it comes in as a thought, a word, etc. understanding how you're getting the information and giving it as you're getting it will help the flow of the reading. You don't want to be scattered in your delivery. Lock and load what you're getting so that it comes out clearly. The sitter is not in your mind, so they are not processing the information in the same way. In fact, you are receiving the information in pieces. It's up to you to take those pieces (like a puzzle) put them together to create that image/ message for your sitter. Give them the pieces and build a story around it so that it creates a fluid connection with spirit. You always want to build on that natural psychic connection that is the goal.

Interpreting relationships

One of the most challenging aspects within a reading is accurately determining the relationship of the spirit stepping forward to your recipient.

There are times when you may misinterpret the relationship. Perhaps you feel a mother coming through, when in fact, it's a grandmother. This is common because you may be interpreting the essence of the role they played in their sitter's life or how they *felt* towards your sitter, instead of the true lineage bloodline. For example, if it was a grandmother who raised the sitter then they absolutely may feel more like a mother coming in rather than the grandmother because they assumed that motherly role. Another reason could be *fear.* You have a young girl as your sitter and although you feel a *mother* in spirit, your logical mind chimes in to say *"she's too young to have her mother in spirit"* so you go to the safer bet and say *grandmother.* This has happened to everyone at some point in time.

How can you accurately decipher and discern the relationship of a spirit to the sitter? It's about practice and learning to understand how the relationships feels within your own body. Once you hone and understand how those relationships feel within your own body then as you're connecting to spirit you tune in to feel where that spirit resonates within you. This will assist you in determining that relationship more accurately. Using your clairsentience, you can make your own body a reference and establish the sensations of various family members within your own physiology. Think of it as having special ring tones for various family members. A grandmother has a ringtone (sensation), father, mother, etc. Establishing how these various members *FEEL* within your own physical body will help to trigger the feeling within.

If you have strong clairaudience, you can also simply ask the spirit what their relationship is to the sitter. Another option is to use your compass. If you get a feeling about the relationship, check your compass for the "yes" or "no". This method works quite well as it will help you between close relationships such as father vs. step-father.

How do you build your accuracy? When you give a relationship to the sitter and its correct, *FEEL INTO* that **YES** from the sitter. How did that relationship feel to you the moment you heard *"yes"*? This will help you build accuracy in discerning relationship.

#1-Sit with loved ones

Sit with spirit with the intention of tuning into you're your family members. Once you are relaxed and focused and have taken a moment to raise your vibration, think of your various family members. Start with your family members in spirit and truly pull in their personality, essence and how they feel within you. Invest in this exercise and relive those feelings, memories and emotions as detailed as you can. See where this relationship sits within you.

Does it feel closer to your heart? Perhaps, your stomach?

Then move to the loved ones in the living and do the same exercise. This exercise will help you start to really tune into getting relationships and personalities in your readings. Furthermore, it will help you to discern who is in spirit and who is still in the living whilst doing a reading. Journal your experience and write out who you sat with and how they felt within you. The more detailed you can be with this exercise the more effective it will be.

#2-Family Tree

In this exercise you will create a type of family tree. Using your own physical body as the tree, you will establish where each family member resides on this tree. For example, you may wish to place all females on your left side or may choose to put all maternal family members on your left side. You can switch this and have males on your left side. Choose what feels more *natural* to YOU. Once you establish this element, then move on to hierarchy. You may want to place grandparents at the very top of each side (so off to your upper left or right). Followed by parent's underneath, then aunts and uncles may be extended off of your parents slightly. Your siblings would be equal to you with cousins extended out. Perhaps children are lower and pets being the lowest since they are the closest to the ground. You can establish this tree and hierarchy so that when a loved one steps in you can see where they fit into the tree and work on relationship from that point. This exercise can be done using your clairsentience or clairvoyance as you may see the family tree within your mind's eye.

Here is an example of a family tree. Again, this can be customized to your preference. This particular example has maternal relatives placed on the left and paternal relatives placed on the right, but you could arrange it placing all women on the left and all males are on the right or vice-versa, etc. There are many options and **NO** wrong choices.

FAMILY TREE

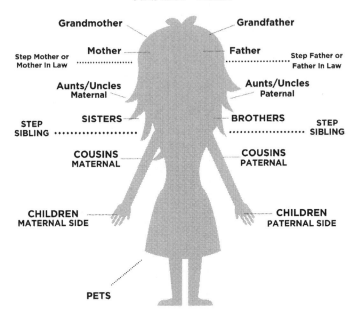

Grandmother

Grandfather

Step Mother or
Mother In Law

Mother

Father

Step Father or
Father In Law

Aunts/Uncles
Maternal

Aunts/Uncles
Paternal

STEP
SIBLING

SISTERS

BROTHERS

STEP
SIBLING

COUSINS
MATERNAL

COUSINS
PATERNAL

CHILDREN
MATERNAL SIDE

CHILDREN
PATERNAL SIDE

PETS

Interpreting Memories

When doing a reading you may have a memory come forward. How do you know if that memory is from spirit itself or if you are picking it up directly from your sitter? The best way to determine where the memory is coming from is looking at the point of view. If you start bringing forward a memory and the sitter is letting you know that you are describing their personal experience to a tee, including how *they* felt then, more than likely, you are connecting to the sitter psychically. However, if you are connecting directly from the spirit, your memory will be from the *spirit's point of view*. Your sitter may not connect fully to the experience of the memory because it's not their perception of that particular memory for them.

Here's an example:
Let's use an example of two sisters. One sister is in the spirit world and the other is in the living. The sister in spirit tells you how they would go to plays together, but she always hated plays. She went for the sake of her sister. She'd rather be out dancing, but she loved her sister so much she went for her.

When you start to say to the sitter "I'm being shown plays, but you hated them and only went for the sake of your sister" the sitter would say "NO, that's not true, I LOVE plays", in this moment take a beat to realize that you are being shown the perception of the spirit, the spirit is referring to *HER* experience and *NOT* the experience of her sister, the recipient.

That's when you realize your interpretation is off a bit and you can rephrase it as follows:

Medium: *"Would you understand that your sister may not have enjoyed the plays, but always went when you asked her to go?"*

Sitter: *"Oh my goodness, yes I do. I had to drag her out with me, but she always went for my sake."*

Medium: *"Well, she's letting me know she would have preferred dancing."*

Sitter: *"Yes, I can absolutely see that, she always wanted me to go dancing! Lol!"*

When you are trying to determine who is giving you the memory and where that memory is coming from simply look at the point of view.

Another interesting element is that spirit may be giving something that feels like a memory to you and you deliver it as such, yet in reality it's something that the sitter has recently done themselves in their own physical life. In this case, the spirit is simply letting you know that they witnessed it and are trying to show the sitter that they are still around and providing evidence of their continued existence.

Here's how this may be delivered during a session.
Let's assume you are being shown a vase of roses by a Grandmother in spirit. You immediately interpret that as the Grandmother giving her roses at some point.

Medium: "Would you understand a vase of roses your Grandmother gave you?"

Sitter: "No."

You then have to go back to the spirit and interact with them. Ask them "Are those your roses? Did you give them to her? Does she have them?" -*Engage* in conversation with the spirit. In this case, the grandmother tells you that they are on the table.

Medium: "Would you understand having a vase of roses on a table in your home, would that be correct?"

Sitter: "Oh, Yes, I didn't think of that!"

Medium: "Your grandmother is letting me know that she knows you recently purchased these roses and put them on the table so that you know she's around you.

A third example is bringing through someone you believe to be in spirit, but they are still in the living.

As the medium you begin to describe the spirit of an older woman who is ill and in the hospital. You see family around her praying and rosary beads being held.

The sitter says, *"that sounds like my mother, but she is still in the living"*.

Here's where you take a moment to go back into your clairvoyant image. From whose eyes are you seeing the images? Did you see them from the older lady? Were shown looking up at people as if you were in a hospital bed yourself or were you shown an image of being above and looking down at the lady in the bed?

If your point of view is looking down at the lady in the bed, then it's someone else in spirit you are connecting with and they are referring to that person. You then have to go deeper to see who is with you.

If you are looking up *FROM* the eyes of the lady in bed herself, then you are connecting directly to her soul.

If you are above, then ask who is showing you the lady? Perhaps she has a spouse in spirit, or another loved one wanting to simply let the sitter know that she is there with loving support.

These are examples of how the point of view will show you *who* is giving you the information, the evidence, the detail and who it's for. This helps to decipher whether or not it's a psychic link or a medium link. How do you get it right? Through practice and experience. You start with tuning into the spirit and simply engage with them. When you get a no or it's not connecting, don't shut down, simply peel the layers away to see if you somehow misinterpreted what you received and try again using the above recommendations.

CHAPTER 15 |
INTRAVENOUS DRIP

What is the intravenous drip? If you've ever done a reading connecting to spirit and the information suddenly stops, you have experienced the *intravenous drip.*

This is when you sit and wait for spirit to drip the information directly to you.

A common misconception is that spirit will give *YOU* all of the information without you needing to do anything but *"be open"*. However, like any conversation, it's a *TWO-WAY* street. Most times you will sit and wait for spirit to give you a piece of information and then you deliver it to your sitter. This works fine for the first few minutes, but then it suddenly drips in slowly or stops altogether. You begin to pause, stutter and feel as if you've lost the connection. At this point, your confidence begins to waiver and you are hoping the floor will open up and swallow you whole! Your monkey mind starts to chime in with taunting remarks like *"Who do you think you are?"*

Does this sound familiar to you?

However, have faith because the connection is *not* lost, you're just ignoring it. Instead of having spirit do all of the work for you, it's up to YOU (yes YOU) to be proactive and interact with spirit in the same manner as you would sitting across a table from someone and chatting over a cup of coffee.

It's similar to any relationship and any conversation. There has to be an exchange of energy between YOU and the SPIRIT. You are not just a messenger; you are a medium!   You must be pro-active and interact with the spirit. Initiate a question, be curious and ask them about their life. Do they have a family?   Do they have children? Did they have a good life? When they respond to you with a yes or no, go DEEPER! Be genuinely curious to get to know them.

Here's an example of a two-way conversation with spirit:

Medium: *"Do you have children?"*

Spirit: *"Yes"*

Medium: *"Wonderful, how many?"*

Spirit: *"Two"*

Medium: *"Oh you have two children? Boys? Girls?"*

Spirit: *"Lucky enough to have one of each."*

Medium: *"That's wonderful! I bet you loved them dearly."*

Spirit: *"Yes, I sure did, I loved our camping trips where we'd tell ghost stories!"*

Medium: *"Camping? You took them camping, huh? Oh, I bet they loved those stories."*

Spirit: *"Yes, we'd try to outdo one another with the best story. In fact, my son just told one of those ghost stories to his daughter the other day."*

Now, here's how *you* relate this to the sitter who happens to be the son of the father.

Medium: *"I have a man here who tells me he is your father. I would be correct that you have a father in spirit?"*

Sitter: *"Yes, I do"*

Medium: *"He's letting me know that you have a sister as well, correct? He wants to acknowledge both his children."*

Sitter: *"Oh wow, yes, I do have a sister, that's amazing."*

Medium: *"He's bringing me to a memory of taking you all camping. You would understand camping trips with your father and the family, correct?"*

Sitter: *"Yes, we loved it."*

Medium: *"Your father is telling me about the ghost story contests you would have around the fire!"*

Sitter: *"Oh my goodness, I can't believe it. YES, we did it and he loved that."*

Medium: *"In fact, He's telling me that you just told your daughter a ghost story the other day."*

Sitter: (getting emotional) *"How do you know that? Yes, I did tell her!"*

Medium: *"Your father is sharing this to let you know that is he still around you and loves that you are passing along his favorite family tradition."*

See how this flow of conversation brings forward incredible detail, memories and evidence from the spirit?

In this simple exchange you were able to determine relationship, validate children and how many and the gender of each. You were also able to validate a granddaughter *and* bring in a specific memory *and* show the sitter that the spirit is still around them by giving an instance of something that happened *after* the spirit has passed. This is all within a few exchanges. Imagine, what could come in with a full session and conversation with spirit!

Allow yourself this interaction and conversation with spirit. Remember to stay relaxed and in the

113

moment with spirit and commit to being authentically connected to the experience with that spirit will allow you to be curious and inquisitive.

One of the most important aspects to remember when doing a mediumship connection is to simply have a conversation with the spirit. You don't want to get into a space of interrogation while you're asking the questions. As previously mentioned, you want to create a very natural flow and if you are genuinely curious about that spirit and allow yourself to be present in the moment to tune into how that spirit feel and really see, feel and year what they are giving you, then you will be able to deliver the information in a very relaxed natural manner. This is how you bring forward the essence of that spirit to your sitter. This can only happen when you trust your connection. You don't need to rush the information. The information will unfold as you lock and load and deliver it in a way that tells a story that will be well-rounded. Your sister will feel the experience of their loved one in the room with them. When you work with spirit remember they are a person. They were in the physical world (just like you) and when you remember that important detail and talk to them in such a way that honors and respects that, you will see a reading that unfolds like a beautiful story with meaningful messages.

If the intravenous drips returns, take a second and go back to where you felt strong. Go to where you received the last "yes" or two and rebuild it from there. Repeat those validated points to help raise the vibration and then interact with the spirit to bring in the next piece of evidence that they would like to share with the sitter. If you need, take a sip of water as that will help to raise your vibration. Doing this back and forth creating a natural ebb and flow of connection and communication with the spirit. This simple method allows you to connect with that spirit on a more personal and intimate level. You will be able to talk about subjects and bring forward information that is special to that spirit. This may be a memory or something they wanted to share something that they've known that has happened to the sitter since they've transitioned. All of these things will help tight in that relationship that connection and bring forward a much stronger link with the spirit.

Conversation Exercises

Exercise #1

Invite an acquaintance to a coffee shop (not someone you know too well) for the sole purpose of getting to know them. If you have a friend's mom or a friend of a friend, this would work best. Sit across the table from them and have a genuine conversation. Notice how you are inquisitive and courteous to your guest. Take note to how you naturally will ask them a question based on a piece of evidence they just shared with you. Be mindful of how you naturally build on this. This exercise will show how to have a conversation with spirit.

Exercise #2

Refer back to the example in Chapter 9 using the compass and the grandfather's watch. Using this example, write out 10 possible questions you could ask the *grandfather* personally about his watch? These questions should be conversational. This exercise will help you to expand your imagination and be more conversational with spirit.

Exercise #3

Do a medium reading in which your goal is to merely have a conversation with the spirit. What evidence naturally comes through? How did the experience feel for you? Were you able to feel connected to the spirit and their life? Were you able to share this conversation with the sitter in a way the sitter could relate to and resonate with? After the session, think back to the session and write out 10 questions you could have asked that spirit in building a stronger conversation with them?

CHAPTER 16 |
MULTIPLE SPIRITS

What do you do if you have multiple spirits coming in together during your reading? How do you discern between the different spirits? Would you even know if you had more than one spirit?

In all fairness, it's not always clear that there's more than one spirit with you especially when you're beginning on your journey. You may feel that you only have one spirit and it isn't until you start delivering the information and evidence to the sitter that they may say something like "oh, that sounds like *both* my grandmothers". Normally, this may make you feel as if you've failed or haven't connected. Don't let this discourage you. You simply need to go deeper and discern who is who in your connection.

For example, you may say something along the lines of "I have a lady here who is letting me know she is your grandmother. She loved to knit scarves for the family and had to have her hair done at the salon every week."

Your sitter may respond with "OH, that sounds like a combination of *BOTH* my Grandmothers".

You then take a breath and deliver another piece of information and the sitter says, "that sounds like *Grandma A*". You then give another piece and the client chuckles and says, "*that* sounds just like *Grandma B*". At this point you want to give up and doubt your own connection but STOP the negative self-talk, roll up your sleeves and trust you can do this! Know that this can be absolutely normal because they *feel* as one to you, but you can separate the spirits and discern and connect to each one individually and build a strong link to each spirit individually.

"*How do you do that you ask*?" Great question!

Once you are made aware that there is more than one spirit, in your mind's eye place one spirit on your left side and the other on your right side. Separating them in your mind's eye will help you separate the information and evidence that's coming forward. This allows you to simply focus on the energy and soul of one spirit at a time. Turn to *Grandma A* who've you put on your left side and find out who she is, what is her personality like, what was her relationship like to the sitter, habits, mannerisms, memories, etc. Don't be afraid to dive in deep and be sure to validate the information with the sitter. Set your intention and focus to only connect with her in this moment and bring forth everything she is about and represents.

Once it's affirmed and you've given the evidence and information and finish that connection you can then simply turn to your opposite side and address *Grandma B*. Treating them as individuals will help you get specific details and evidence.

What do you do if one spirit is "quiet" and they "aren't saying anything"? Tune in to see if the spirit is actually showing you their personality by their silence? Were they reserved and quiet in the living? If so, you can't expect them to be a Type A extrovert in the spirit world. Are you engaging enough with them? Maybe they said something or gave you an image and you glossed over it so they feel you aren't listening? Pay attention to both what they *DO* and *DON'T* give you. This is *key* in the communication.

There are many times when more than one spirit will step in, but of those, one may stand further back or off to the side. Sometimes this is simply to show support. They are not in need to necessarily delivering a message, but to simply represent. Other times it may be because they feel they need permission from the sitter to step forward. This may happen if the spirit had done the sitter harm in the living or if there is shame connected in any way. If this happens, always acknowledge that spirit to the sitter. When you do this, that spirit may step forward at that point and begin to communicate or they may choose to simply remain in the background. Either way is fine as long as you're are engaging with the spirit to determine which of the two it may be for them and honoring it.

Here's an exercise that you can practice helping you sensitize your feeling and build your clairsentience to *feel* when a different spirit steps forward.

EXERCISE:

Think of a loved one in spirit. This could be anyone you wish. For example, your grandmother. Feel her step in very closely. Spend time with her. Talk to her. Then ask her to bring in another loved one for you. Feel the energy changes as this one steps in. Feel the vibration of their personality. Does the energy feel different to you? Take notice of all of the nuances. Now go ahead and talk to this loved one. After a few minutes, pause and go back and talk to your grandmother again. Switch back to the loved one she brought in for you. This will help you start to understand the changes in your own energy and the feeling when different loved ones step in for you.

Piggybacking

Piggybacking is a term used to explain when two or more spirits step forward simultaneously giving similar evidence but are usually for different recipients. Typically, because the spirits are so similar in their details and evidence, the medium perceives them to be only one spirit. The medium may deliver pieces of evidence and two (or more) recipients raise their hand and can take *ALL* of the information as given by the medium. In some instances, this can become a sort of tennis match between the two spirits and the recipients as the medium attempts to deliver a piece of evidence that would differentiate them and solidify the proper recipient. This frequently occurs more in a group setting, circle or platform demonstration in which there are several potential recipients in the audience.

Why does piggybacking occur and how to you resolve what sitter the spirit is for?

There are several possible reasons why piggybacking occurs in a public forum.

At larger events, there will be too many attendees to realistically have everyone receive a personal message. Spirit is infinitely intelligent and understands this so behind the scenes they begin partnering up in an effort to get as many of their messages to their loved ones as possible in the allotted time. As a result, you may have two mothers in spirit who have similar personalities and circumstances, so they come in together. Think of it as a type of streamlining from the spirit world to be as efficient and productive as possible

The medium proceeds to deliver the information and zero in on the proper recipient. If more than one recipient takes the information, the medium will deliver another piece of evidence in an attempt to hone in on the correct sitter. If both attendees continue to take each piece, it can go back and forth several times becoming a sort of tennis match. This can sometimes lift the energy of the room as the audience begins to engage in the match itself. If the back and forth continues but to no avail, then at some point the medium must simply go back to the spirit and ask, *"Who are you for?"* and let the spirit indicate who they are for.

As the medium, a good indicator is to look at your feet. What direction are you standing? Where are you facing? Spirit will naturally shift your body in the direction they are trying to get you to go. By being aware of your own physical body you allow yourself to open and then may feel who the recipient is for or notice where your body is naturally leading.

Ultimately, the goal is for the medium to narrow it down to the correct recipient and deliver the message. As the medium, always thank those attendees who participated in the piggybacking and raised their hand. Never disregard a participant after you've determined your true recipient. Be gracious to your audience and thank them for their time and energy.

Many times, a medium will believe they have piggybacking when indeed is merely a lack of detailed evidence. Delivering general or vague evidence increases the possibility of multiple recipients being able to take the information. If you encounter this situation, go for more specific evidence to narrow it down to the correct recipient.

Another factor could be that you have a sitter in such grief they will take any piece of evidence as theirs because they desperately want to hear from their loved one in spirit. As the medium, it's your responsibility to serve for the highest good and ensure you are connecting the right spirit to the right sitter.

Lastly, who is to say that the spirits aren't doing it intentionally to make sure each of them is "heard"? Referring back to mothers again, let's call them Betty and Diane. Betty and Diane decide they each need to desperately speak to their daughter as she's been going through a terrible time. Knowing it's unlikely they will both get through with messages, they decide to tag team and come in together. They each give the medium a piece of evidence and the medium delivers it. Betty may be saying to Diane, "Ok, Diane, your turn" and so forth. Even though they both know the message will ultimately be delivered to only one recipient, they know by doing this, that *BOTH* daughters will *know* and *feel* their mother present with them and that was all these mothers wanted to convey. This spirit mission was successful because each mother accomplished her objective!

Overall, as you continue to build your connections with more readings and gain experience, it will become easier to discern when there's more than one spirit present. Once you start recognizing the feeling of more than one spirit present, your clairsentience will trigger each time more than one spirit steps through to communicate.

VARIOUS SPIRITS AND VIBRATION

Along with learning to discern how to handle when more than when spirit is stepping in together, there is also the discernment between a child, animal, adult, guide or angel. Each spirit holds its own vibrational level. In very much the same way a radio has different stations and frequencies so does the spirit world.

Children and animals will come in with much lighter and buoyant energy because of their innocence and unconditional love. They didn't live from ego.

Guides and Angels have even a higher vibration because their frequency which is why you must raise your vibration even further to connect to them.

By building your clairsentience you can start to establish how the vibration of each "type" of spirit feels within your aura. This will help you to determine if you have a child in spirit, a beloved pet over the rainbow bridge or you're connecting to a sitter's guide or a loved one.

CHAPTER 17 |
SIGNS AND SYMBOLS

Signs and Symbols can serve as a wonderful tool when connecting on either a psychic or medium level. Many psychics and mediums use signs and symbols to help in their communication and interpretation of the information they are receiving. A sign or symbol has a representation, a meaning attached to it. As the lightworker, you would catalog your signs and your symbols and set a particular meaning to them. Perhaps you are shown a rose and a rose would either represent a relationship of a family member, such as a grandmother. Perhaps, it represents someone's name. It could have a literal meaning of an actual rose or rose garden. It may simply be a symbol for a token of affection or love. The meaning behind the rose is unique to the psychic or medium. As you cross paths with signs and symbols you can develop your personal encyclopedia of their meanings. Each time you receive a sign, or a symbol ask yourself *"What does this mean to me?"* The important aspect is not to go with what *everybody* else thinks it means, but to be true to what meaning it represents for you. This is important so when Spirit or your higher self is trying to connect and communicate, they will use those signs and symbols to create a form of dialogue to convey those messages to you.

Another example would be a key. Many people feel that a key represents opportunity or a new car, perhaps a new home. There are others that would see a key as representing success. A key could symbolize a new beginning, letting go or a need for safety and security. As you can see a simple key has many possible explanations as to its potential meaning. This is why understanding what this means to you will help you connect it to the recipient as it becomes a form of language. Many psychics and mediums will use these signs and symbols to also validate to a sitter that their loved ones in spirit is connecting with them and giving them those signs and symbols as a way to show them they are present.

When connecting on either a psychic or medium level, always go with the literal meaning of a sign or symbol first. You would be surprised at how often there is a literal meaning rather than a figurative one attached to that sign or symbol. A lot of readers will immediately jump to a symbolic meaning first out of fear that their logical mind has played a cruel trick on them by giving them something unique. They tell themselves "that can't be real, it must be a symbol". Perhaps you see an eagle and you think it's not possible the sitter has an eagle or any connection to one, so you immediately change the reference to "I see an eagle and for me that's my symbol for a new sense of freedom". Take a chance and *FIRST* say. "I am seeing an eagle." "Would you understand the connection to an eagle"? Internally and simultaneously ask your compass, *"Do they have a pet eagle?", "Did they save one?", "Are they an eagle scout?".* "Are they an Eagles football fan?". By having the courage and willingness to put it out there directly, you are learning to trust your connection and that literal meaning may just be something like *"Oh my goodness, we saved an eagle we found last week and felt such joy when we were able to help it fly away"*. Perhaps there is a loved one in spirit that was showing you the eagle to let you know that they are aware of this random act of kindness that their family did, and they wanted to make sure they knew they were still among them.

Options are endless with signs and symbols and what they could mean, but with practice and attunement, you will be able to discern if that sign or symbol is literal or figurative. You will also learn how to determine if it's from someone in spirit or connected to the sitter in a more psychic capacity. Each time you see something that catches your eye, have a thought about what that means to you. Lock and load that internal response and catalogue the meaning as you move forward. Establish as many signs and symbols as you can to help you convey the messages of those loved ones and of the higher self. Below are a few exercises to help you create your symbol encyclopedia, however it's important to remember to always go literal first when conveying the image you are being shown!

SYMBOL JOURNAL:

Keep a journal and start to log if you have symbols that pop up for you and write the symbol and the meaning. Start to build a catalog of any symbols that you see. Keep this with you during the day.

SIGN MEANINGS:

Copy the image below and use it as a practice sheet. Next to each image, write down the first thought that pops into your mind about the meaning of that symbol. If you really want a bit of fun, make a few copies, pass them around to friends and do it together without looking at each other's answers. You can compare your sheets and you may just be surprised at how different the answers can be for each of you!

Symbols & YOUR Meaning to them

PART 4

Responsibilities

CHAPTER 18 |
GETTING PERMISSION

You have your sitter in front of you and you are eager to start your psychic link. You are ready, but STOP! There's one crucial step that needs to happen before you begin.

One of the things that's so important to do is to ask your sitter if they want to know *everything*. Getting permission from your sitter is absolutely *required*. Your sitter has the right to refuse information they are not ready to hear.

TWO-FACTOR PERMISSION

The 2-factor permission is a responsible way to ensure you have checked in with your client properly. The first of the two-factor is verbal permission. Ask your client to give you a verbal YES or NO as to whether or not they are open to receiving ALL of the information that comes through or if they prefer to only focus on certain aspects.

The second of the two-factor is non-verbal. This is where you tune into their soul to see what your sitter's soul can handle. Even though they may have just said yes to you, you may, in return, give them something that is just too much for them to handle at this point in time. Think of this as a 2-factor authentication security check we see in the internet world. How many times do you have to put in your user ID and password to only receive a 6-digit code via text message that needs to be input before accessing your account information. Essentially, this is what we are doing, but on a *soul* level.

Honesty and integrity are imperative to this line of work. If we're going to help elevate the standard and reputation than we must elevate the way in which we deliver information we are receiving. Starting with a verbal yes or no, then tuning into their soul for a second security check to see what their soul can handle allows us to not cross any unwelcomed boundaries.

An experienced nurse will continuously check the blood pressure of their patient to ensure that various doses of medication aren't triggering the pressure to go too high or too low. We want to condone ourselves with the same level of ethics and responsibility. Our job is to take care of our sitter by creating a safe place for them to feel the love and support they need at that time. This is an important reminder in the work that we do as we are not serving ourselves but rather, we are serving the universe and spirit.

CHAPTER 19 |
PROJECTING

When giving information, there is a natural fear of "What if I'm making this up? Is this all just in my head?"

In reality, it should *ALL* be in your head! This is your imagination tapping into the vibration of psychic and mediumistic frequency. However, if you're using your own fears, blocks or opinions to deliver information, this is called projecting. We want to avoid projecting at all costs as it's not being of service. We never want to pass judgment onto our sitter.

Our goal is to truly honor the information coming forward in an unfiltered way. It should be so authentic and clear as you channel the information. In order to do this, you must check in with yourself.

If you hit a stumbling point, ask yourself "is this my opinion or from source?" Many times, spirit will give us the guidance we personally need through our sessions so it's understandable that we may confuse the two at times. In a reading, don't allow your ego to step in. We want to be of service at the highest vibration possible.

CHAPTER 20 |
VOLUNTEERS NEEDED

One of the best ways to practice your psychic gifts is to find volunteers.   Volunteers are willing participants open to a reading from you. Let them know that you are practicing. Share that you are simply doing it from a place of learning and growth. When you find your volunteers, ask that they only give you a simple *"YES"*, *"NO"* or *"I DON'T KNOW"*. You don't want a sitter to give you too much information. If they do, then they will be doing the work for you.

Be mindful of reading for family and/or friends. Sometimes in the beginning phases of your development it's difficult to find volunteers except for those that are closest to you in your life, however, this can become a trap as you grow. If you start reading for friends and family, they will want you to continue reading for them. This can interfere with the relationship. Try going out with a friend for dancing and all they want to know is what is going to happen in their relationship! Sometimes our friends and family don't want to hear the truth and if we give it to them, it can cause friction within the relationship. If you choose to allow your friends or family to volunteer, set clear boundaries up front. If you can find a development circle or an online circle, this may be the best way to find the volunteers you need.

Remember, to implement the two-factor validation and that you don't make decisions for the sitter. Share with them that your intention is to simply expand and develop your gifts in the purest way possible. Always thank your sitter for being a volunteer as they are allowing themselves to be vulnerable to you during your growth.

Most importantly, *please* don't go around trying to predict a person's passing for them or their loved ones. This is an unethical practice. If something comes in so strongly you have to infer what that means, do it with compassion and empathy. We always want to work with the highest level of ethics and never create fear around the work that we are doing

Now as you have your sitter in front of you, you will want to go into those areas of importance as discussed earlier. Don't be afraid to push yourself. Don't be afraid to go for it. Challenge yourself. Don't hold back. Now, go have fun with your volunteers as many are very excited to have you give them a reading!

CHAPTER 21 |
GETTING NAMES

How do you work on names? Do you tend to put a lot of pressure on yourself to get names in a reading? Giving a name can absolutely validate the information. Yet, it's important to remember that the information comes in many different ways. You may not see or hear a name within your connection. This is *100%* OK! There's so much more to evidence than just names.

However, if you do want to try to work on names or any specific details within a reading you have to practice!

Here are some exercises that you can do to help develop your ability to call in names during a session. Think about all the people around you and their names. Write them down. Include the names of all the people you know with your friends, family, work place, acquaintances, etc.

Consider unusual names as well but practicing names will help bring them into your reference. Your reference is like an encyclopedia for spirit. They will use the information in it to assist you in making connections. The more you can add to your encyclopedia the more spirit will have to pull from during your time together. In a psychic reading, you get information, but it's also pulling from your own reference. How do you reference the information? It may not be a name that you've heard before, but if it's similar to something you've got then that will help that name will pop in.

Practice names from generation to generation. Pull up your ancestry and look at your own family tree. What names are popular per generation or by gender? Use your family tree to go back several generations. This will help to familiarize yourself with common names associated with specific generations and geography.

Another exercise offered by Lisa is to sit down with a timer and write as many names as you can in a minute. Put the timer on and in one minute put the letter A and write down as many names that begin with the letter A as you can in this minute. You can then proceed to do it for B-Z. Additionally, you can segregate it to only female names and then do it again for only male names. Again, this practice will help significantly bring them into your awareness and store them in your internal encyclopedia.

With each reading you do, tell your sitter you are practicing names and then set the intention for a name or two to come in and be courageous in giving it to your sitter. If you have to "think" and then a name pops in, this is probably your logical mind and the name won't be accurate. However, if you relax with the intention and a name simply "pops" in gently, that will usually be more of an actual link and increase your odds of accuracy.

The above exercises are relevant for any details you wish to work on during your readings. Practice it. Play with it. Don't try to perfect it all in one session. Practice one specific thing at a time. Let yourself build your psychic connection in a naturally organic way. If you do it all at once you will only get overwhelmed and feel pressured to "get it all right". Taking your time to perfect your detail gives you the highest sense of hope and imagination. This allows you to feel relaxed and that is key in building your psychic gifts.

NEXT STEPS

Want can you do to help expand and develop your gifts further? You always have the practice exercises so do them regularly. Also, when the time is right, consider reading for volunteers, but disclaim to them that this is only during your practice phase. Focus on one aspect you want to develop further. For instance, names only. Or it could be what kind of shoes they preferred to wear and why?

Consider answering these questions when documenting. "How were you getting it?" "How is it coming in?" "Did you see it, hear it, feel it or simply know it?"

CHAPTER 22 |
SELF-CARE

In this chapter we are going to discuss the importance of self-care. Self-care is an integral part of working with your highest vibration and the connection with spirit.   As we raise our vibration and sustain that vibration at a certain level, it can start to drain our energetic battery. Think of it as solar power. If it's cloudy, overcast and rainy then the power is not recharged. It needs the energy of the sun to replenish the power.

We have three "batteries" that must work together in order for us to be at our maximum our energetic capacity. This is our Mind, Body and Spirit. Each is an essential component of our battery. As a result, we need to replenish and recharge that battery on all levels to move through any of the negative energy or toxins that we may absorb while working with our connection and our highest vibration.

Just to be clear, there's no negativity when working with spirit, the negativity comes with simply holding the space of that of others and absorbing their fears, emotions, anger, sadness, confusion and other emotions. For example, if you are connecting psychically to someone and you pick up on their fear or worry, by being an empath or having that connection you may absorb some of those similar feelings which then need to be removed from your physical body.

Working with this higher vibration you become a sponge. In some ways a sponge is wonderful because this allows you to blend with spirit, but the same as a sponge absorbs everything that comes into its pathway, your physical body reacts in much the same way. At times it may even impact your mind and spirit. You will absorb those lower vibrational emotions of fear, anger, worry, etc. and this may leave you feeling depleted. The drained feeling needs to be cleared away so that you may maintain your highest vibration and be a clear vessel for working with others and spirit.

What are some of the ways that we can practice self-care? First is to imagine self-care as our mind, body and spirit. Simply focusing on one area alone and expecting that to suffice as self-care won't work. Self- care is a sense of balance.

Some of the ways to work with self-care in our physical body is to indulge in nature. Perhaps a hike, walk along the beach, rock climbing or camping. Spending time in nature will help you naturally connect directly to source.

As we get busy in our lives we forget about nature. We ignore it and find excuses to put it on the back burner.

Here are some ways to get back to nature:

- Hug a tree
- Listen to the sound of birds
- Walk along a beach
- Go for a hike
- Breathe in the fresh air
- Try rock climbing
- Camp outdoors (your backyard counts)!

All of these will help you replenish, find balance and integrate self-care to your physical body.

Here's **THREE** wonderful exercises you can do in nature giving you an opportunity to practice self-care AND your clairvoyance and clairaudience.

1. Go for a couple jogs or walks this week in nature (on a beach, hiking, etc.). As you are jogging your goal is to notice *10* things in nature around you utilizing ALL of your senses.

2. On another walk or job, take notice of 10 things you SEE in nature. Then once you are finished, recall them in your minds' eye with vivid detail. This will help you expand both your physical eyesight and your mental eyesight.

3. On your third day, notice 10 things on your walk or jog that you HEAR in nature. Again, at the end of the job, stop and recall with detail the sounds you heard. This reinforces the outside hearing with the inner hearing.

Classes are also extremely beneficial to your self-care. There are many types of classes, simply find

one that resonates with you. Here are a few
suggestions to inspire you:

- Yoga (Hot, Bikram, Hatha, Vinyasa, et al.)
- Meditation
- Spinning
- Dance (Try taking salsa or ballroom!)
- Breath
- Drumming circle
- Singing

Any class that allows your physical body to move
the energy through it will be productive and
restoring.   Dance, music and singing are all
wonderful ways to raise your vibration as well.

In response to focusing on self-care with your
physical body, you will be reconnecting with your
higher-self. This new energy and movement will
naturally negate and purge any of lower vibrations
that have found their way into your physical body.
Massage is also another fantastic tool to move
energy through your body. Additionally, Reiki and
Acupuncture are also great sources to utilize.
Anything that facilitates the blood flow, oxygen,
muscle and energy will help in removing old or

negative energy in your chakras. For example, let's say, unbeknownst to you, you are holding onto something in your heart because you did a reading for someone with a broken heart. Somehow, your empathic self has held onto this pain. Moving the energy through you removes and pushes away those negative emotions which is why taking care of your physical body is essential.

Self-care is also essential for your mind. According to the *National Science Foundation*, the average person has approximately 12,000 to 60,000 thoughts per day. Some have countered that it can be up to 70,000 a day. Shockingly, they found that an estimated **95%** are *repetitive* thoughts and of *those* thoughts approximately **80%** are **negative!** **NEGATIVE!** This is what we refer to as little ego and it can absolutely hinder your connection if not managed properly.

If your mind is filled with thoughts and worry you will have a difficult time focusing and allowing the clear channel of spirit to step through. This is why working on mental self-care is so important. Meditation and creativity are integral to the process of self-care. Meditation is a discipline and practice that when done regularly can minimize your mind chatter, creating an open vessel to connect to your higher vibration. This results in an easier connection for you and for spirit.

Creativity is also very helpful in self-care. When you're drawing, painting, coloring, singing, dancing, writing or any activity that allows your creative mind to activate, you are expanding your awareness. These practices will absolutely help you with self-care because it's feeding your soul and creating the balance necessary for a strong connection.

Laughter is also an amazing tool to help you with self-care. Laughter has several health benefits in addition to naturally raising your vibration. When laughing you are automatically clearing any fear or negative thoughts from your system. It's literally impossible to feel sadness, depression, anger or resentment while actively laughing. You can soothe that stress away with a good old-fashioned giggle. Laughter can give you a fresh perspective as well. With increased energy and less stress, you will begin to feel less overwhelmed and more confident of your connection.   RX of the day: Laugh, Laugh hard & LOL!

Another component of self-care is caring for your own soul. A wonderful way to practice this is by giving back. Donate your time and your energy to causes that feel in alignment with you and do it in a way that respects and upholds your boundaries. When you give back through charity or simple random acts of kindness, you will find that your soul feels at one with itself. We are meant to be here to help one another and love one another. When we remind ourselves of that and when we practice that we are in essence, engaging in self-care.

We will discuss boundaries in a later chapter, which is absolutely essential to self-care. Learning to say "NO". In summary, self-care is comprised of the mind, the body and the spirit. For the body, you want physical activity, movement, flow and nature. From classes to activities, get that body moving and allow that energy to flow through you. Massage, Reiki, Acupuncture, Crystal Healing, Salt Baths, etc. also moves the chi through the body. With the mind you want to clear that space in an effort to keep an open vessel. Free from negative thoughts or mindless mental chatter. Self-Care with the soul is practicing anything that makes you feel fulfilled. Meditation, Automatic Writing, Creativity, etc. The options are endless as there is no "right way" to honor your soul, but to listen to what it needs.

Another important reminder of self-care is to seek proper medical care when needed. If you are sick, DO NOT wait it out. Take care of yourself and go to your doctor. Taking care of yourself is imperative to your well-being, longevity and spiritual connection.

CHAPTER 23|
SELF-LOVE

Are you feeling tired? Exhausted? Find yourself burning the candle at both ends? Many times, we tend to take care of others before we exercise our own self-love. This can leave us feeling isolated and frustrated with our friends, family and co-workers. We start to question our purpose and path. One of the greatest gifts we can give others is to love ourselves first.

When our tank is full, we have more to give to others. We will be more patient, listen more intently and give more freely. When we commit to practicing self-love, we create inner and outer peace for ourselves.

When working with your highest self and the vibration of spirit, it's absolutely imperative to maintain strong self-love habits and routines so that you stay healthy both physically and mentally. If you are not at your best, it will be a struggle to maintain strong connections for any extended period of time. Additionally, when you help others connect to their true self, you want to encourage self-love on their journey. You won't be able to do that if you aren't reflecting it in your own life.

One of the best ways to integrate self-love into your beliefs is to practice! By practicing consistently, you will fall into a natural state of self-love. It won't feel uncomfortable or awkward. It will simply feel in alignment!

Negative Self-Talk Exercise

Spend one full day being fully aware of your negative self-talk. What negative words do you find yourself using? What pressure have you been placing on yourself? Each time you find yourself saying a negative, being fully aware, stop and turn that sentence into a positive immediately. We are energy and the universe is energy. How you speak to yourself directly impacts how you allow others to speak to you.

HERE ARE 8 AMAZING EXERCISES TO FILL YOUR *LOVE* TANK!

1. Write a poem to yourself

Put pen to paper and write yourself a nice little love poem! It can be as simple as this:

"ROSES ARE RED, VIOLETS ARE BLUE, NOBODY LOVES YOU AS MUCH AS I DO."

2. Write 5 examples

Explain with 5 examples how you've grown *spiritually* over the past year.

3. Look at yourself in the mirror and repeat the following:

- *I am a good person*
- *I deserve to love myself*
- *I deserve true love*
- *I deserve to be financially abundant*

Reminding yourself that you are worthy and there is no need to settle will help you make the choices that are for your highest good. The choices that reflect self-love the most.

4. Remove the word *CAN'T*

It's easy to default to negative language. When we change our words, we change our thoughts. Start by removing the word CAN'T from your vocabulary!

5. Pat yourself on the back

Literally. Tell yourself you've done a *GOOD* job at the end of the day! We tend to be so hard on ourselves. We plow forward without ever taking a moment to reflect on what we have accomplished. Take a few minutes at the end of the day and take gratitude for what you DID accomplish!

6. Stop yourself

In the middle of chaos, stop yourself and say, **"I've got this handled".** When we are stressed, we lose focus. Our thoughts get cloudy and our decision-making skills decrease. Instead of getting frazzled, get it handled. Remember: *You got this!*

7. Post positive affirmations

Write down a few yummy soul feeling affirmations on sticky notes and post them on your refrigerator. Create a practice in which you cannot open the fridge until you read them. They will serve as reminders to keep your thoughts positive and your vibration high. They may just be the "pick me up" you need!

8. Write

Write a list of your top 3 accomplishments this past year. By remember what you've done, you will be inspired to do more.

Confidence

As you develop your gifts, your confidence may waiver. There will be times in which you are filled with self-doubt. There may even be days in which you simply want to give up. It is in these times that you must dig deep and get *"gritty"*. When you doubt, think back to an experience in your life (spirit related or not) in which you nailed it. It went exactly as you had envisioned. Take a moment and feel that within your body once again, embrace that and then bring it into your current situation. This will help you move forward. NO ONE can give you confidence. DO NOT seek approval from others. Find the courage to move past your fear and remind yourself that spirit would not be placing you in this position if they did not believe in you. You've spent most of your life hiding your gift, trying to live "normally" in a chaotic world.

Let go of living the life others want for you and live the life that resonates within you. If you have the calling to help others and facilitate healing in any way possible, own that as your purpose and make that your mission. Success starts with believing in yourself and never cower. Get back up when you fall down. This is YOUR experience so don't waste your energy trying to please everyone around you. You are amazing and this world needs you so never dim your light for the comfort of others.

CHAPTER 24|
BOUNDARIES

Upholding personal and professional boundaries can be difficult, but a critical necessity for working with the energy of people and spirit. Many lightworkers tend to be nurturers, empaths and people-pleasers. This is one of the many qualities that draws them to the energy and vibration of others. However, there will be those that want to take this energy from you. This isn't necessarily in a manipulative way (although in some instances, this may be the case), but very similar to how a moth is drawn to light.

You are the light and there will be those that want a piece of that spark, the energy you have to offer. If you don't work on upholding your boundaries, you will become exhausted and drained to a point of jeopardizing your physical health. One of the most important words for you to learn is "NO". Now, let's practice this together.

On the count of 1-2-3....."**NO**"!

If something does not feel right to you or you are too tired to give of yourself, don't be afraid to say "NO". Some around you may resist or retaliate, but over time, your friends, family and clients will learn to respect your boundaries. This gives you the freedom needed to stay energetically healthy and strong.

7 WAYS TO SET BOUNDARIES

1. Reflection: *Review your past year. Take a look at your relationships.*

Are you feeling fulfilled in them? What about your own boundaries? Do you sometimes feel that you're an easy "doormat" and yet, you can't seem to find a way to give up on people?

Allow yourself permission to take a look at whether or not someone is bringing joy to your life or are they adding stress?

We can find ourselves staying in situations long after we know it's over. We *know* it's not healthy. Why? Why do we stay? Perhaps it has to do with not giving up on someone or wanting to look at "their" side of a situation, a belief that "this is the best it's going to get" or a fear of change.

Set a boundary that works for **YOU**! Listening to the advice of a friend or family member can lead you in the wrong direction because they will be working from their perception. It's important for you to work from your personal point of view. Take the time to connect with yourself to see what *FEELS* right to you. If it doesn't *FEEL* right, that is a boundary. If it **DOES** feel right, then you know you want to work in that direction. Be your own compass.

2. Set your Boundaries: *Now make a list of your new boundaries.*

Start with creating a list. Look at all of the areas in your life. Love, Relationships, Career, Finance, and Health. Ask yourself in each of those areas do you feel fulfilled? Do you feel a sense of joy? If the answer is NO, then focus on that area. Write down what you are feeling. Then write down what you *do* want. Find a way to simply phrase what you desire. That is part of your list!

3. Uphold your Boundaries: *Stand strong for what you want.*

Having the courage to set boundaries and the discipline to uphold them can be difficult. It's important to implement boundaries into your life as it tells the universe what you feel is your "self-worth". In order to attract from the universe what you truly want, you must be specific in telling the universe what that is for you. So many people leave it up to the universe to guess for them! Do your part of the work and allow the energy of that to respond to you.

Are you the type of person who is constantly giving someone 2nd chances, or bending the rules or pretending something didn't happen? Does that make you feel good? Do you feel loved? If yes, then keep doing it! If the answer is *no*, then release the need to keep giving. By being honest with yourself, you can change the types of people, situations and energy your draw in. The more you can honor your boundaries, the more joy you can bring into your life.

4. Apply Boundaries to all areas: *Love, Work, Health, Money, Relationships.*

Boundaries can apply to any aspect of your life. If you're feeling underappreciated at work, look at what you're volunteering to take on. Do you say **NO** to new projects? Or do you continuously take on extra tasks because you're afraid of upsetting the boss? Using your **NO** can become your new best friend. There's nothing wrong with expressing that it doesn't feel good to you. If that upsets them or you lose friends because of it, trust that it's the universe's way of guiding you to what is in the best interest of your highest self.

Be sure to look at the areas of your life. Let's say it's *Love.* You've been seeing someone, yet it's not going where you want it to go. You say to yourself "oh, they just need more time" or "they'll come around". The co-dependent might say "if I just love them enough".

Stop for a moment, ask yourself this. How do **YOU** feel? Are **YOU** ready for a commitment? Yet this person isn't responding? Then you have to tell the universe, that you want a commitment. The universe will either respond with having him have a change of heart or removing this person from your life. Either way, the universe will set you up to bring what you're asking from it.

5. Be Gentle with Yourself: *It's a learning process.*

If you're a people pleaser or a nurturer then being firm in your boundaries can be especially difficult for you. You have a tendency and desire to appease everybody. You may put your spouse and children first and then there's nothing left in the tank for you. Time to change that. And know, that you may not get it right the first time. You may find yourself slipping into old habits even *AFTER* you set those boundaries but be gentle. It takes *time* to recondition yourself.

As you begin to honor yourself above all others, you will find a renewed sense of energy, curiosity and passion again for the things you enjoy the most!

6. Listen to your Inner Compass: *Surrender and let it guide you!*

Once you focus on listening to your inner compass and following that, you will find a level of authenticity because you will no longer have to "fake" it in a conversation or relationship. The people you start to attract into your life will naturally have the same core belief system. As we change, our circle changes as well. As a friend once said, "maybe you just haven't found your tribe yet". Put yourself out there! Your true and authentic self, and then see who is in *your* tribe.

7. Be Honest: *Honesty really is the best policy!*

Being honest with ourselves and others can be a challenge at times. We don't want to upset someone or hurt their feelings, so we decide to settle. We tend to keep our mouths shut. You are doing a disservice to yourself by enabling this behavior. You are not being authentic to **YOU**. Why must you always be on the back burner? It's time to be honest. Those who are meant to be in your life will still be there with you.

Listening to your inner self and setting boundaries can be risky. If you honor your boundaries, you will create change. That's how it works. You must be open and ready for change. If you are to draw into your life what you truly desire, this is the way to do it. There may be some bumpy roads as people don't like change. You may even find yourself separating from friends, jobs and relationships. However, if you are being honest in your quest, you will find a sense of peace, joy and respect for yourself that makes it all worth it!

CHAPTER 25|
ETHICS AND INTEGRITY

in·teg·ri·ty the quality of being honest and having strong moral principles; moral uprightness.

This topic is so critical to the path of a lightworker that it's been adapted here again from *Leap of Faith: How To Build Your Spiritual Business*. Ethics and Integrity may be difficult to define because your personal experience and perception comprise your overall belief system. In an industry constantly plagued by allegations of fraud and charlatans, the public is craving legitimacy. People *want* to believe, and as a healer in the new world, this is your opportunity to elevate the standard. By accepting responsibility for your part in revolutionizing the perception of the metaphysical industry, you can contribute to creating a shift that reveres lightworkers with the same level of credibility and respect as doctors, teachers, accountants, scientists, and lawyers.

How many times have you seen a doctor walking around a grocery store giving a diagnosis to the customer in the produce aisle? Probably not too many, right? Avoid the temptation of giving readings or healings to random strangers you meet in public. It's these practices that have triggered apprehension among the public. Some of you may be thinking *"but I can't help it, spirit won't leave me alone."* Practicing as a professional is having the control to "turn it off" when you're not working in that professional capacity. Through discipline and training, you will find that you do have the ability to refrain from delivering a message.

In an evolving world of enlightenment, you may not be able to convert the skeptic, but your actions can reflect a level of professionalism resulting in a heightened respect for the industry as a whole.

Create a safe haven for clients to trust and surrender. People will entrust you with their deepest fears, secrets, and desires; please take this honor as a privilege and provide them with a protective and safe environment conducive for healing.

Delivering Messages

Delivering a message can be a complicated endeavor at times, especially when there is a tragedy and sudden loss surrounding the loved one. It is imperative to handle the message with integrity. The client will carry what you say about their loved one with them *forever*. They will cling to your words; from their perspective, it's the last bit they have of their beloved. There is an obligation to "give what you get" and be the true "medium" of spirit, but it can be handled with grace and compassion. Imagine if someone told you that your loved was "stuck" and unable to transition fully to the other side and that it was your responsibility to help them.

Can you fathom what that would feel like?

There's story from a client who had gone to a pet communicator after her precious "Trixi" had passed away. The pet medium told the client that Trixi was "stuck in a green jelly" and that the client "had to figure out what the dog needed" so that it could fully transition. This is a person who loved her dog like a child. She rescued, pampered and spent thousands of dollars on medical treatment to give this fur-baby the best quality of life possible. Words can traumatize and scar a client. Being mindful of our words and messages can take a session from the most traumatizing to the most healing simply by being caring and compassion in how the message is delivered.

What if you are out and about enjoying a nice dinner and spirit pops in with a message for the patron next to you. Do you deliver it? Or perhaps your getting a psychic hit for a friend or family member, do you call them to tell them?

This is tricky ground and should be looked at on an individual basis. You can't say that it's NEVER ok to deliver an impromptu message as there are times when spirit will want you to step in on their behalf to deliver a message. However, this is rarer than not and as a psychic or medium, it's your responsibility to not continuously be so open you are constantly receiving messages. Set your "hours" with spirit so you know when you are "on the clock" and "available for service" so that you can also have a normal life of enjoying a dinner without distractions.

However, when there are times that you feel that nudge so strongly, start off with saying something very casual to the patron next to you. Don't dive right in and ask them if they want a reading. If they seem to be receptive, share what you received, but don't start going deeper and giving them an entire reading at the restaurant. Again, this will only cause discomfort. Keeping it quick and simple will surely get the message across.

For friends and family, be cautious about giving them insight and messages. As previously mentioned, this might be a necessity in the early stages of development, but as you grow, this part should be strictly enforced to preserve your relationships. If you are constantly giving your family messages, you will strain those relationships. Simply tell them, *"I'm sorry, but I am no longer reading for friends and family."*

Avoid Gossip

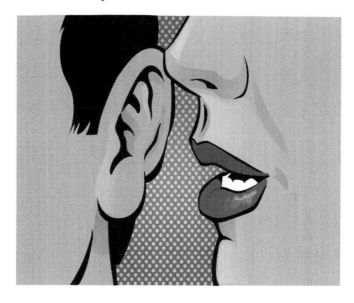

Along your journey, you will encounter many other healers. There are guaranteed to be some that you prefer over others but remember to always be respectful to all. Maintaining strong relationships is vital to your growth. If you hear whispers among peers regarding another light-worker, simply refrain from engaging. When in doubt, ask yourself what would you be willing to say to the person directly? What if they could hear your conversation? Focus on building connections with others so that you have a community to collaborate with and shy away from words or actions that don't come from your highest self.

When in doubt, remember The Four Agreements by *Don Miguel Ruiz*.

The Four Agreements:

1. Be impeccable with your word.

2. Don't take anything personally.

3. Don't make assumptions.

4. Always do your best.

— **Miguel Ruiz**, *The Four Agreements: A Practical Guide to Personal Freedom*

Upholding Client Boundaries

Upholding boundaries and exercising ethics are another element. Be cautious of becoming too intimate with a client. If a close relationship develops, ask yourself if you are truly working for the person's "highest good" and in the name of spirit. Working as a professional requires understanding your boundaries and limits as a light-worker. If you choose to continue a personal relationship, consider referring them to another light-worker for future professional sessions.

This holds true for friendships as well. If you know every little detail of a dear friend's life, withhold the temptation to read for them. We may all need a little insight or advice here or there from our friends – that's normal, but refrain from engaging in full sessions. There's a conflict of interest and with any solid professional, we want to avoid crossing that boundary at all times. There is an ethical duty in this work, and we must make an oath to ourselves and spirit to work responsibly.

Avoiding Substances

Don't work under the influence of alcohol or other substances. You wouldn't want a doctor performing a surgery while intoxicated, so handle your own profession with equal standards. The same holds true for a client. If they arrive for an appointment intoxicated or under the influence of drugs or other substances, refrain from continuing the session. Their judgment is impaired, which goes back to creating a safe and protective environment.

Diagnosing

As previously mentioned, avoid dispensing medical diagnosis, treatment or prescribe medication unless you are legally authorized in your area.

Setting Limits

Set a limit as to how many times you agree to see a client within a particular time period. Some clients can become addicted to healing, guidance, and readings; it's up to you to set the boundaries. If you state the terms and include them within the policy on your website, you will always have something to refer back to should you need to inform a client you are unable to work them. You can also explain that time is necessary for the energy to manifest; therefore, you will see them again within *X* number of months.

Research

Never research a client prior to a session. It may be easy to get wrapped up in the stardom of a client or succumb to the pressure needing to be accurate but trust your gift completely. If you don't get a name or every perfect fact, this is a GOOD thing! Trust what spirit gives to you. If you research, google or Facebook, etc. you are jeopardizing your reputation and dishonoring the integrity of spirit. Trust your gift and know that spirit will provide.

BONUS EXERCISES

Here are a few additional exercises to help you practice, play and develop your gifts further.

SYNCRONCITIES:

EXERCISE 1
Angel Messages

Spend a day noticing every number that pops forward. Keep a notepad with you. Every time you see a number (or series of numbers like 555) write them down. Be aware of license plate numbers, totals on receipts, numbers that catch your attention.   Write the numbers down in the order you get them throughout the day. This is *why* the notebook is important.

At the end of the day, take the numbers and look each of them up. This website is a great resource:
http://sacredscribesangelnumbers.blogspot.com/p/index-numbers.html

Write out a message from spirit only using the meaning of the numbers as you are interpreting them. What is the message you get by piecing the numbers together?

Look at each number individually and take it on an individual journey, not a general overall message.

For example, you get a 7, 10 and 13. "*This would be that you are in a phase of spiritual enlightenment. That you are opening your psychic abilities and that you are able to manifest your fits and to further develop your personal spirituality. (this is the 7)

Understand that you create your own reality. You are receiving guidance from your angels at this time but pay attention to your own intuition and it's time to take positive action towards those feelings. You are stepping into a new direction and this is time to have faith that you are on the right path (this is the 10). Allow yourself this expansion and growth and to feel the optimism and excitement around this new beginning. Again, this is about trusting your intuition.

You may experience some upheavals at this time, but this is for lessons that will help you to help others" (this is the 13). —In essence, you give yourself a reading based off of the 3 numbers you saw.

Meanings -Courtesy of sacredscribesangelnumber

EXERCISE #2
I Spot Synchronicities

Write out number 1-99 on small pieces of paper that can be cut and folded individually. Please these in a jar or can and give them a good mix. Each morning upon waking, reach in and pull one number from the jar. Look at that number. Your mission should you choose to accept it is to look for that number throughout your day. Try to see how many times you can spot it. This will help you realize the power of synchronicities and how spirit will continue to give you signs, symbols & messages.

AUTOMATIC WRITING, CHANNELING & MEDITATION EXERCISES

EXERCISE #1
Discover your gift

Sit in a quiet place with your journal. Sit and ask spirit "What would you like for me to discover about my gift?" Open your eyes and begin to write. Don't worry about proper grammar or spelling. Don't focus on the words but the intention. Write for 5 minutes and then read what spirit gave you.

Exercise #2
Break free from blocks

Sit with spirit in a 15-minute meditation with the intention of asking spirit about any BLOCKS you may have. In this meditation ask them about the blocks and how you can clear them. Write out what you are given in an automatic writing exercise.

Exercise #3

Fear of Love

Do an automatic writing exercise (sometimes this is best while playing a song). Set the intention of answering the question: "Why am I afraid to let people love me?" Write out your answer without filtering the response from your higher self.

Exercise #4

Channel Spirit

This is a channeling exercise in which you will sit in a quiet space and allow yourself to relax. Set the intention to ask spirit "What message would you like to give about true love?". Open your journal and begin to write without stopping. Allow the words from spirit to flow onto the pages. Write for 5-10 minutes. Upon completion, read the message spirit gave you.

Exercise #5

Spirit Goals

Sit in meditation with the intention of asking spirit to give you the 3 top ways in which they would like for you to be of service. Understand this can change and fluctuate over time so don't stress over this exercise. It's merely to allow you to realize that you can connect and communicate with spirit directly their goals and intentions for you.

Exercise #6

Sit in the Power

Sit in the power for 20 minutes at least 3 times in one week. While sitting in the power, allow your body to fully relax. Use your breathe to raise your vibration and allow the flow of energy to move from your feet through your body and allow it to soar through the top of your head. Allow your aura to expand during this experience.

The goal of this exercise is to fully own the power of your soul. Own your all-knowing source. Feel oneness with the universe. Describe in detail your experiences. Elaborate for each one separately. List the day and time you did this exercise.

Psychic Exercises

Exercise #1
Dream Weaver

Keep a journal of your dreams for one week straight. Write down every dream, the date, time and detail as much as you can remember. If a dream wakes you up, write it down before you go back to sleep. Start to take notice as what is coming through your dreams. Are you having premonitions? Are loved ones visiting you? Are you seeing something in your dream that then shows itself to you while awake? Be as detailed as you can to watch how your subconscious is working to help you open your gifts.

Psychic/Mediumship Exercises

Exercise #1
Connecting to Spirit
Find a volunteer that you can do a 30-minute medium only reading. Let them know this is purely a development assignment. They must know their loved ones very well. Sit with spirit and focus on truly blending with that spirit using your clairsentience.

Allow yourself to be vulnerable and have them share the space with you as you bring forth their personality, memories, habits, etc. Remember to go into the stages of a reading, but the focus is on fully surrendering and *BLENDING* with the spirit world. *Remember* to make it conversational with them.

Exercise 2:
Bite Size Spirit

Look for volunteers and do readings in which your objective is to only focus on *ONE* aspect such as:

Personality
Habits
Memories
Names
Favorite Hobbies
Relationships
Appearance
Occupation

Exercise #3
Stage Break Down

Do a 30-minute reading where you spend the first 20 minutes ONLY focusing on HARD facts then move to SOFT facts and spend 10 minutes here. Finally, move to the MESSAGE and spend 5 minutes here.. Keep each stage separate for the sake of training. Spend the last 5 minutes bringing them all together.

Exercise #4

Brown Bag Spirit

Have a friend or colleague take a photo or memento of a loved one in spirit for them and place it in brown paper bag so you can't see it. Do not let them tell you who that loved is to them. Do not feel this bag, allow your hands to gently touch the bag to then tune in to the spirit and deliver the information to your sitter for validation. This is a fantastic exercise in trust and surrendering.

Exercise #5

Psychometry

Psychometry is a psychic exercise using your clairsentience to tune into the energy of a material object for the sake of bringing forth evidence and delivering information. This may be an item of someone in the living or in spirit. It may have been passed down. Find a volunteer that will allow you to hold that item and give them a reading about the impressions you are receiving. Are you getting clairvoyant images? Are you connecting to a loved one in spirit for them? (*Even if you connect to a spirit, you have made that link psychically as you*

199

used an item to then link to the spirit, rather than spirit initiating the contact with you).

Ask your sitter for validation. Remember to relax, trust and *ALWAYS* handle your sitter's beloved item with the absolute care with ease and love.

Conclusion

There is no limit to how many times you can read this book or repeat the exercises. Developing your gifts is a practice not a destination. Don't be afraid to tell your friends, family and community about your gifts. This is YOU. Some of you may live in smaller towns or suburban areas where this line of work is often looked upon with a skeptical eye. Or, perhaps you come from a background that frowns upon spiritual work. It's time to start looking at yourself as the one who can help change the perception – and in the process, transform lives. If you do this with intention and authenticity, your light will shine. Start believing in yourself and let spirit guide you.

There will be times when you are fearful; please know that this is NORMAL and OK, but you must have the courage to push through it in order to reach your goals. When you have moments of doubt and concern, take a deep breath and surrender.

When you are challenged, you grow. Each time you try something new or give yourself the permission to step into your path, you are growing. More than likely, you've been in the spiritual closet for many years. With the door closed, no light can get in or shine out. It's time to turn the knob, open the door, and let your light shine brightly. When you step out of the closet and into your power, your world will become brighter because you are finally embracing your gift and purpose.

ABOUT THE AUTHOR

Colby Rebel is an international psychic medium, certified master spiritual teacher, radio host, #1 best-selling author, and public speaker. She has endured vigorous testing and is a *Certified* Master Spiritual Teacher of both psychic and mediumship development through the Lisa Williams International School of Spiritual Development in Los Angeles, California (LWISSD), having been personally invited to the program by world-renowned psychic medium *Lisa Williams*.

Colby is a *certified* Advanced Psychic, and Advanced Medium through LWISSD. She has also studied at the acclaimed Arthur Findlay College in Stansted, England. Prior to taking the *Leap of Faith* to build her own spiritual practice, Colby worked in public accounting and taxation for fourteen years. Colby has been featured on several television programs demonstrating her gift of spirit.

She shares her experience and knowledge for the purpose of giving you the direction, inspiration, and tools you need to understand and develop your own spiritual gifts.

She currently resides in Los Angeles and is the proud owner of the *Colby Rebel Spirit Center* where she teaches and sees clients on a private basis.

FURTHER READING

Ask Your Guides*: Connecting to your divine support system-Sonia Choquette*

The Alchemist -Paulo Coelho

So You Want To Be A Medium? -Rose Vanden Eynden:

Droplets Of God: *The Life and Philosphy of Mavis Pittilla* -Suzanne Giesemann

Paul, Man of Spirit: *The World of Paul Jacobs* by Jenni Gomes

The One Thing -Gary Keller with Jay Papasan

The 50 Secrets of Self-Confidence -Richard Nugent

The 5 Second Rule -*Mel Robbins*

The Four Agreements*: A Practical Guide to Personal Freedom (A Toltec Wisdom Book) -Don Miguel Ruiz*

The Survival of the Soul and ***I Speak to Dead People Can You?*** -Lisa Williams

Oprah's Master Class Podcast -Oprah Winfrey

VISIT COLBY
www.colbyrebel.com

Colby is available for keynote speaking, consultations and seminars on the topics of building a successful spiritual business and mental success. She also conducts workshops on spiritual development including intuition, psychic and mediumship.

More ways to connect with Colby:

Email: **Info@colbyrebel.com**

FB: **https://www.facebook.com/PsychicRebel/**

Twitter: **twitter.com/PsychicRebel**

IG: **www.instagram.com/psychicrebel**

READY FOR MORE?

Colby offers pre-recorded trainings to help you develop your psychic and medium gifts. You can watch these in the comfort of your own home on your schedule. Build your skills and download today!

VISIT: www.colbyrebel.com/courses/

If after reading Psychic Senses you are ready and motivated to take your gifts to the next level and have a desire to serve in a professional capacity.

Leap of Faith
How To Build Your Spiritual Business
By: Colby Rebel

www.amazon.com/Leap-Faith-Build-Spiritual-Business/dp/099665318X/

"Colby is a "medium's medium" in other words, she is one who encourages, supports and promotes other mediums in a selfless way. She is an excellent medium in her own right demonstrating throughout the world and undertaking private sessions. She is also a modern medium utilizing social media very effectively both for herself and others, even hosting her own radio show. I am proud to know her, to have worked with her in the past and I hope to do so in the future. She is what all mediums should aspire to be.

-Mavis Pittilla, *World Acclaimed British Medium, Former AFC Senior Tutor and Ambassador to Spirit*

Made in the USA
Middletown, DE
03 August 2020